The Circumcised Heart of Love

by Robert B. Henley

Servias Ministries Press
P.O. Box 1471
Bethany, OK 73008 U.S.A.
www.servias.org

Manufactured in the United States of America
ISBN 978-0-615-34895-7

Cover art by Bonnie Snapp Blount
Interior layout by Sarah Leis

*This book is dedicated to Pamela
and her unconditional love for me.*

Table of Contents

Foreward

On February 18, 1972, I proposed to my wife using 1 Corinthians 13:4 as a basis for our marriage. Needless to say, I was unable to live up to those precious words for I was young and immature. Over the next thirty-seven years Our Heavenly Father has been patiently molding me into a man who is now beginning to understand HIS Love. Many people claim to know HIS Love but few walk it out. Don't judge this book by my actions but judge it according to the actions of Jesus. He is our example. My quest is to walk accordingly and only do and say what I hear from Our Heavenly Father. The globe is in need of this revelation. Without it, men will continue to wage wars, control the masses, and lord over those who know no different. The Scripture speaks of a millennium of peace but in order to get there, Love must prevail. This is what this book is all about.

Robert Henley, 2010

Introduction

PREPARING THE HEART FOR LOVE

*D*aniel 12:4 "But you, Daniel, shut up the words, and seal the book until the time of the end; many shall run to and fro, and knowledge shall increase."

Printed information is doubling about every four years. Biological science's knowledge is doubling every 180 days. A study claims by 2010 the amount of digital information in the world will double every 11 hours. At the time of this writing the world is dealing with wars, famines, possible financial chaos, health epidemics, and political upheaval. With all the increased information, we would expect the opposite but that is not the case. As the Internet expands across the globe, more people are seeking out information and knowledge but without results. Yes, we can find many answers to our day to day needs, but what are the answers to our major societal dilemmas? People have substituted information in place of revelation. Revelation is the disclosure of the truth about a matter. Facts only provide details without the complete understanding of how those facts tie together.

The truth provides a clear understanding of facts and intent. More information is not the answer, revelation is!

My goal in writing this book is about revelation, not just information. If you simply want more information, go to the library or surf the Internet. If you are seeking revelation about the "big picture" as I am, read on. None of us has all the answers. We are to supply each other with our piece to the puzzle. Many have sought the Face of God hoping to achieve a higher level of understanding and relationship. The Old Testament provides many stories, patterns, and prophecies all pointing to the glorification of the Temple. Men yearn to see the day when The Lord's glory re-enters the Temple. Many have predicted the return of Christ and were wrong. The predictions continue. Are you fully prepared for the "Return of The Lord"? In my quest of preparation I have sought The Lord, studied the Scripture, read books, listened to tapes, analyzed Bible names and numbers, and conducted exhaustive word studies. Even though I have studied Biblical topics for that past 37 years, I view myself as a student, not an expert. The prophets had one thing in common—revelation.

Luke 2:49-50

49 And He said to them, "Why did you seek Me? Did you not know that I must be about My Father's business?"

50 But they did not understand the statement which He spoke to them.

What is Our Heavenly Father's business? I believe He is in the business of love. That is what this book is about.

Part One:

THE SWEET SIXTEEN

Chapter 1

LOVE IS PATIENT

*T*he first characteristic of love mentioned in 1 Corinthians chapter 13 is patience. In the Old Testament the term "slow to anger" described patience. Patience is the state of tolerance, steadfastness, or endurance under difficult circumstances, delays, or provocation without becoming annoyed or upset; or exhibiting forbearance when under strain, especially when faced with longer-term difficulties. Patience is tied directly to "overcoming", as a man who is not diverted from his deliberate purpose and his loyalty to faith by even the greatest trials and sufferings.

Most Americans have lost the characteristic of patience. Fast food, technology, and prosperity have promoted the "Now Generation". The focus is on the speed at which one can obtain something. Patience works through the problem rather than submitting to an alternative action. Marriage requires patience. The dramatic increase in divorce is often tied to impatience although the popular reason for divorce is money. Money is the symptom not the reason. Young married people want everything NOW because they do not understand patience and growth. Their egos suggest they should have bigger houses and better cars before they can truly afford them.

Persistence is a characteristic of patience which establishes an unwavering and reliable focus. Others can count on your consistent commitment which facilitates development of relationships. This requires sacrifice by both sides in a relationship. Paul states in Romans 12: 1, "I beseech you therefore, brethren, by the mercies of God, that ye present your bodies a living sacrifice, holy, acceptable unto God, [which is] your reasonable service." In the twelfth verse "patient in tribulation" is mentioned as an attribute of being a living sacrifice.

Patience is in direct conflict with lust. Lust craves for immediate gratification. Lustful desires redirect our attention to an act of empty results. Patience is test of endurance and endurance is an attribute of growth and maturity. If we habitually succumb to the lustful desires of the flesh, our love suffers.

James 1:2-4: My brethren, count it all joy when ye fall into divers temptations; Knowing [this], that the trying of your faith worketh patience. But let patience have [her] perfect work, that ye may be perfect and entire, wanting nothing. (KJV)

Patience is developed by the "trying of our faith" and has a direct correlation to time. No one relishes going through trials even for a short period of time let alone an extended period. In the Old Testament we find many tests of faith spanning years. Abraham held on to a promise even when most of us would resign ourselves to the assumption of failure since our promise did not happen by the end of the day or week. As babies we had come to expect our needs to be met immediately by a simple cry or whimper and as toddlers our nagging proved somewhat successful. As adults we are to put away childish things.

Our problem is that we don't understand the big picture. The Book of Job was a classic example of this "continuum" that we live in. Consider the following Scripture:

Job 1:1: There was a man in the land of Uz whose name was Job; and that man was blameless, upright, fearing God and turning away from evil. (NASB)

How many of us can claim an introduction similar to Job's? Job knew The LORD and The LORD knew Job. It was Job's custom to rise up early in the morning to go before the LORD and offer sacrifices on behalf of his family. How often do the fathers get up early and pray on behalf of their families now? Job was blameless, honest inside and out, and he feared or reverenced GOD thus there could be no better man to be found in the land.

All was going well with Job and suddenly all hell broke loose for the adversary, the devil, had been allowed to test Job. The Sabeans killed his servants and stole his asses and oxen just as a fire consumed another group of servants and sheep. At the same time an additional group of servants were slain and the camels taken. To top it all off, a great wind or tornado struck the house of his sons and daughters killing them. I guess the nickname "Lucky" does not apply here.

What was the purpose the story? I do not know one person who would want to go through the trials of Job and suffer through all of his tests. He lost most everything dear to his heart and the legacy he created was virtually destroyed. Did these tough times mean that his name would be removed from the local university business administration building? Job had an unconditional love for Our Heavenly Father, he had walked uprightly with a pure heart, and he had turned away from evil. What more could be asked of him? Ultimately, love will be tested and patience is the first attribute mentioned by Paul.

When things are going well, it is easy to walk in love. However when the trials and tests arrive, real love endures. The trials and tests reveal what is in your heart and even after all the bad news arrived, Job sinned not nor charged GOD foolishly.

The next test came as health problems as once again the adversary had received permission from GOD to further test Job. This time his three friends show up to provide their view of the problem: Eliphaz the Temanite, and Bildad the Shuhite, and Zophar the Naamathite. When they arrived, Job's pain was so great thus they remained silent for seven days and nights. After the week of silence the four of them began to logically figure this problem out. Surely Job did something wrong! Maybe GOD just woke up on the wrong side of the bed. Was the ultimate calling of Job to suffer and die after having all that he had worked for be removed? Job regrets his birth and wishes that he had died at birth. He longs for death. Job and his friends have a lengthy discussion about Job's problem. Each makes his case to Job about the source of the problem and they reason with Job about the various aspects of life.

Job tried to interpret the events as punishment, as a lesson, a need for sacrifice, yet nothing changed. He was attempting to use the logic of cause and effect as the reason for his situation. What did he cause that created this effect? Why do the righteous suffer while those workers of iniquity seem to flourish?

Finally Our Heavenly Father speaks to Job and begins asking him questions about the universe. Job is asked about the stars, the sun, and Job's inability to understand the various aspects of nature. I'm sure that is not the answer Job's brain was looking for. Our logic looks to performance not just being a part of some vast plan. Our Heavenly Father has a magnificent, grand plan of which we are a part. We are called to endure with patience although we may not fully understand the trials as we proceed through them. As we begin to comprehend that the motivation of Our Heavenly Father is love, we can rest in those trials and pursue a response of Love rather than judgment and/or bitterness. We must accept the fact of good and evil as we move through life.

Patience allows you to see what is in your heart and is normally connected with a span of time. In the Old Testament, the words patient or patience were rarely used. Instead, "slow to anger" or "longsuffering" were used to depict Our Heavenly Father's willingness to let an expected outcome develop. How does anger and patience connect with each other? Jesus became angry as we see in the following passage:

Mark 3:5: and when He had looked around at them with anger, being grieved by the hardness of their hearts, He said to the man, "Stretch out your hand." And he stretched it out, and his hand was restored as whole as the other. (KJV)

Jesus was grieved by the hardness of the Pharisees' hearts and responded with anger. The hardness in their hearts developed over time until they became of little use to their fellow man. Instead of ministering life, they allowed death to creep in to the point where the man with the withered hand could not receive healing.

Patience expects a positive outcome in the midst of trials, tests, and tribulations. Patience is developed by walking through or experiencing the trial, not being removed from it. Today, people tend to believe they are entitled to live without any trials and tests. "When the going gets tough, they're gone!" Our egos want immediate gratification which sets an expectation that there is not enough time for us to receive everything we desire thus promoting a base level belief that eternity does not really exist. On the other hand, patience challenges "time" and the belief that it is a scarce resource.

How does anger play a part in patience? Jesus became angry yet at the same time he walked in love. Tilt! How can you walk in love and be angry at the same time? Paul wrote:

Ephesians 4:26: Be ye angry, and sin not: let not the sun go down upon your wrath. (KJV)

Paul was telling us that anger isn't a sin but should not be a sustained response over time. We have all been taught about the "wrath of GOD" attempting to scare us into submission to the pulpit. For us to understand anger in the context of love and patience we must first uncover the purpose of anger or wrath. In the Old Testament, the wrath of GOD was used frequently, 198 times in the King James Version. Wrath and anger were often used with the words "kindled", "fiery", or "wax hot". Anger and fire are tied closely together to provide us a better understanding of the purpose of anger.

In Scripture, fire is a cleansing agent designed to restore, not an act of punishment. Uh oh, did I just step on a sacred cow? Am I saying the colloquialism "Turn or burn" isn't valid? Anger is not revenge but is an immediate response designed to remedy a destructive direction being taken. The ultimate purpose of anger is to correct and restore whereas the purpose of revenge is simply to destroy.

Malachi 3:1-3:

1 Behold, I will send my messenger, and he shall prepare the way before me: and the Lord, whom ye seek, shall suddenly come to his temple, even the messenger of the covenant, whom ye delight in: behold, he shall come, saith the LORD of hosts.

2 But who may abide the day of his coming? and who

shall stand when he appeareth? for he [is] like a refiner's fire, and like fullers' soap:

3 And he shall sit [as] a refiner and purifier of silver: and he shall purify the sons of Levi, and purge them as gold and silver, that they may offer unto the LORD an offering in righteousness.

We see in the passage that fire purges and cleans. It removes the impurities that would prevent us from standing before Our Heavenly Father. Silver is symbolic of redemption and gold represents Divine nature. The refiner's fire is not designed to destroy us but to make us acceptable "offerings" to the LORD.

Therefore righteous anger has its place when taking a corrective action but unjustified anger does not. This is why we must be slow to anger so that as we take on the characteristics of Our Heavenly Father, our anger will be just. Jesus warned us about the consequences of unjust anger:

Matthew 5:22: But I say unto you, That whosoever is angry with his brother without a cause shall be in danger of the judgment: and whosoever shall say to his brother, Raca, shall be in danger of the council: but whosoever shall say, Thou fool, shall be in danger of hell fire. (KJV)

"Without a cause" is the critical phrase in this passage and could be further understood by the translation "without just cause". Who determines just cause? Our Heavenly Father who knows the heart of every man. Patience provides the buffer to our responses that may produce harmful results if acted upon in haste. How many times were we sorry we said something without thinking? How often do we wish we could take back biting words spoken? As we grow in love and patience, our need for repentance diminishes.

Our society is moving away from patience thus promoting impatience. Service to others has been replaced by personal gratification. I want it and I want it now! This "Drive Thru" mentality discourages patience and rewards impatient behavior. Young married couples sacrifice patience for the immediate gratification of owning a big house with two SUV's and a huge debt. On the other hand, patient savers acknowledged their station in life and waited until they had adequate savings and cash flow to buy the home of their dreams. The subtlety of the ego is found in impatient behavior.

James 1:2-4:

2 My brethren, count it all joy when ye fall into divers temptations;

3 Knowing [this], that the trying of your faith worketh patience.

4 But let patience have [her] perfect work, that ye may be perfect and entire, wanting nothing. (KJV)

Patience endures the trials that are set before us and walking in love makes these trials bearable. Love understands the need to be patient as these trials work themselves out. Job received revelation about the "big picture" and that his trials required endurance. Your love walk will become mature as you let patience have her perfect work.

What can we do to promote patience?

- Be still and wait on Our Heavenly Father. Wake up an hour early and just be still and listen. Eliminate outside stimuli and focus.

- Postpone a planned action or purchase.

- Do not immediately and emotionally respond to a trial. Get your emotions under control.

- Practice patience with you family. We all tend to be less patient with them.

- Determine what most often causes you to be impatient and focus on turning it into a strength.

- As you take these steps you will become mature and complete, lacking nothing.

Chapter 2

LOVE IS KIND

*I*n the Love chapter of 1 Corinthians 13, the second attribute mentioned is kindness. This word means "having or showing a tender and considerate and helpful nature". Tenderness is often seen in response to a newborn baby. The child is seen as pure and helpless. The baby can do nothing for itself and must be nurtured. During these first few formative years the child's personality is developed. The baby's form of communication is initially sleeping, gazing, and crying. The cry is the form of communication that alerts us of discomfort. Our challenge is to find the source of discomfort. In kindness and tenderness we eliminate the standard issues. Why do we have such a difficult time being kind to other, older people?

Jesus was kind. What did he have that we don't? He had revelation of man's problem and that revelation allowed him to understand men's motives and forgive them of their actions. His ministry focused on restoration of mankind to our Heavenly Father. He looked beyond the sin of man, the associated actions, and the harsh words from the religious leaders to complete his work on the cross. His kindness had to be greater than the human nature to judge and condemn the people.

The root of the New Testament word "kind" is translated "easy" in the following passage:

Mat 11:28-30: Come unto me, all [ye] that labour and are heavy laden, and I will give you rest. Take my yoke upon you, and learn of me; for I am meek and lowly in heart: and ye shall find rest unto your souls. For my yoke [is] easy, and my burden is light. (KJV)

Is your yoke easy and have you found rest in your soul? Once you have found the fullness of love, you are able to be at rest, your yoke will be easy and your burden will be light. Our quest is to find this place that Jesus spoke about. How can we find such a place of peace and tranquility? We are to pursue this place and sow seeds of kindness so that we can receive the fruitfulness of this aspect of love.

To contrast kindness we must consider the alternatives such as being stiff-necked (stubborn, headstrong, or obstinate). Stubbornness holds on to one's view without considering the other viewpoints. It assumes that the other person cannot hear the voice of Our Heavenly Father. Could the other person be speaking to you on behalf of The Lord since you may have not been listening in a particular area where idols are present? As we consider that each person has specific gifts and callings different from ours, we must consider the possibility that they may be called to connect with us in some way. Our responsibility is to discern the connection with kindness.

Luke 6:35 But love ye your enemies, and do good, and lend, hoping for nothing again; and your reward shall be great, and ye shall be the children of the Highest: for he is kind unto the unthankful and [to] the evil. (KJV)

The Highest is kind to the unthankful and evil. What a doctrine buster! Love does not wish ill will on your enemies, only goodwill. In order to be a "child of the Highest" you will do the following:

- Love your enemies
- Do good
- Lend hoping for nothing in return
- Be kind to the unthankful
- Be kind to the evil

Has your brain gone "tilt" again? These commands go against your ego striving for lordship and dominance. You must not repay evil with evil, but with love. Sorry, these are the words of Jesus, not me. What about the attitude of "Burn, baby burn" in hell? Those in charge of church doctrine needed a way to control the masses and thus a few centuries ago a new doctrine was formed to paint a different picture of righteous judgment.

Goodwill is the proper use of "will" enveloped in kindness. You will then correctly use your will in all aspects of life, caring for others, helping, sharing, and being considerate. You will cease the hurtful actions that have caused division among those in your circle of influence. This goodwill requires strength and determination, a God given strength you DO possess. Just as weightlifting increases your strength through repetition, your acts of kindness build strength and that new strength builds a greater and mature level of kindness.

In Ephesians Chapter 4, Paul provides us with critical detail about our walk:

23 and be renewed in the spirit of your mind,

24 and that you put on the new man which was created according to God, in true righteousness and holiness.

25 Therefore, putting away lying, "Let each one of you speak truth with his neighbor," for we are members of one another.

26 "Be angry, and do not sin": do not let the sun go down on your wrath,

27 nor give place to the devil.

28 Let him who stole steal no longer, but rather let him labor, working with his hands what is good, that he may have something to give him who has need.

29 Let no corrupt word proceed out of your mouth, but what is good for necessary edification, that it may impart grace to the hearers.

30 And do not grieve the Holy Spirit of God, by whom you were sealed for the day of redemption.

31 Let all bitterness, wrath, anger, clamor, and evil speaking be put away from you, with all malice.

32 And be kind to one another, tenderhearted, forgiving one another, even as God in Christ forgave you.

Notice the last verse, "be kind to one another, tenderhearted, and forgiving". Do you think Our Heavenly Father would ask us to be more kind, tenderhearted, and forgiving than Him? As we embrace the character traits of Our Lord, we will begin walking in love and kindness.

Bitterness causes you to be resentful and envious toward others. In Acts chapter 8, Simon (the sorcerer) saw that Peter and the other disciples were ministering to others by the "laying on of hands" resulting in the "giving of the Holy Spirit". Simon then offered Peter money for this gift but Peter discerned what was in his heart and stated that he had a root of bitterness within him and would perish with his money for attempting to buy the gift of God. Here we see the ego in action. Simon had operated in a position of power and dominance over the people by his former vocation of sorcery. Rather than becoming a servant of The Lord, he wanted to retain his power and stature with the local population. Clearly he had been financially successful in his previous work, but now he wanted to continue with the new "power". Simon expected payment in return for his services. Kindness expects no payment in return for its acts. Bitterness prevents you from being kind. You become consumed with resentment about your situation and live in a state of denial, blaming others for your situation. As you distance yourself from your calling, you enter the desert of bitterness. The greater the distance, the greater the bitterness. All you have to do to correct this situation is repent and turn back toward your calling. You will then allow the Holy Spirit to move in your behalf. Get down on your knees and ask Our Heavenly Father to pluck that root of bitterness out of your heart. He will forgive you and with tenderheartedness and kindness He will remove the root and healing will begin.

Kindness is a result of walking in Love and as you seek to be immersed in Love you will see kindness become natural to you. This fruit will be seen by others and they will become attracted to you. Children will sense it in you and will want to be around you. Their sense has not yet been dulled by the cares of the world.

Practice simple acts of kindness. Care for, help, share, and make life work for others. As you do this you will discover the true joy of giving. Acts of kindness to family, friends and strangers strengthen your certainty, understanding, and clarity about what really matters. This enhances the renewal process that Paul speaks of in Ephesians.

Paul urged us to renew the spirit of our mind and to put on the new man by the following commands:

- Speak truth
- You can be angry, but don't let it control you and cause you to sin
- Quit stealing and work honestly so that you can be a giver not a taker
- Speak words of life instead of words of destruction
- Do not grieve the Holy Spirit by your words or actions
- Put away bitterness, wrath, anger, clamor, and evil speaking
- Be kind, tenderhearted, and forgive

Chapter 3

LOVE DOES NOT COVET

*T*he tenth and final commandment Our Heavenly Father gave the Israelites dealt with coveting:

Exodus 20:17: Thou shalt not covet thy neighbour's house, thou shalt not covet thy neighbour's wife, nor his manservant, nor his maidservant, nor his ox, nor his ass, nor any thing that [is] thy neighbour's. (KJV)

Each Commandment, law, and statute is a reflection of the character of the Lawgiver. In your own household, your "laws" reflect your character. Think about it.

To covet is to wish, long, or crave for something, especially the property of another person. When you covet another's possession you are in essence proclaiming what you have and where you are at is insufficient and undesirable relative to that which you seek after. Coveting is deceitful and subtle. In the Garden of Eden, Eve was convinced that what she had was not sufficient and she lacked something. Thus she was deceived.

In the above Scripture, Our Heavenly Father placed great importance on this issue, enough to include it in the Ten Commandments, the cornerstone of lawful, global behavior. Let's first consider your neighbor's house. At the time of this writing the world is in the midst of a financial crisis spurred on by mortgage crisis. What is at the root of the mortgage crisis? Coveting your neighbor's house. People were buying houses they couldn't afford with money they didn't have to impress people they didn't know. Do you think Our Heavenly Father would direct you to get yourself into a mess of this magnitude if you approached HIM with a pure heart? If your earthly father loves you and wants the best for you how much more does your Heavenly Father desire the same?

A friend of mine was a wealthy businessman and lived in a palatial mansion by anyone's standards. There were rooms that cost more to build than my entire house. The house had every amenity you could imagine. The house even appeared in a movie. When I was given my first tour of the house I was awestruck by its majesty and my wife and I were invited to stay the weekend. What a treat! As time went by, I stayed with my friend several times in the mansion on the hill. I noticed something. Each time I stayed, I was less impressed with the house. My desire to stay in the house became less of a novelty and I was no longer awestruck with its majesty. Familiarity breeds indifference. The manifestation of coveting ends in an emptiness that cannot be filled by the object or person being coveted.

Coveting is promoted by an illusion of satisfaction thought to be fulfilling. However, that space needing filled can only be satisfied by Love. Your neighbor's wife cannot fill that void. Jesus made clear His view (and Our Heavenly Father's) of marriage in the following passage:

Mar 10:2-9:

2 The Pharisees came and asked Him, "Is it lawful for a man to divorce his wife?" testing Him.

3 And He answered and said to them, "What did Moses command you?"

4 They said, "Moses permitted a man to write a certificate of divorce, and to dismiss her."

5 And Jesus answered and said to them, "Because of the hardness of your heart he wrote you this precept.

6 "But from the beginning of the creation, God 'made them male and female.'

7 'For this reason a man shall leave his father and mother and be joined to his wife,

8 'and the two shall become one flesh';[fn2] so then they are no longer two, but one flesh.

9 "Therefore what God has joined together, let not man separate." (NKJV)

Verses 7 through 9 have been the cornerstone of the vows in marriage since they were spoken nearly 2,000 years ago. In recent years there has been a shift away from this core Scripture as couples have "rewritten" the vows but this "commandment" remains. Marriage even among Christians has not been based on the solemn vow spoken at most weddings. The Tenth Commandment has been set aside and forgotten just as the Israelites had forgotten their covenant with the LORD.

Our ego once again is at play in all of the issues of marriage. Once we get married, each of us becomes one half of the whole. Why? In Our Heavenly Father's wisdom, HE segregated the duties out between the two. In a marriage, one of the spouses tends to be more logical and the other tends to be more sensitive to the Holy Spirit, sometimes called emotional. In a marriage, you need a double witness of every major decision to insure the optimum result. Being brought up in a household where the man rules the roost, I made many decisions without consulting my wife only to my regret. I finally realized that she was my barometer. If she was not at peace about a decision we simply did nothing and it always worked out. Oh how I wished that I had learned the "Law of the Double Witness" at an earlier age!

What God has joined together, let no man separate! These words of Jesus speak directly to the Tenth Commandment. Man wanted to "work" the Law back when Jesus was walking out His ministry for the hardness of the hearts of the Pharisees provoked the question relating to marriage. There must have been quite a demand placed upon them by men who were seeking an easy way out to divorce their wives.

As we grow and mature in our Love walk, we will no longer be interested in our neighbor's wife. The illusion of satisfaction on the other side of the fence will no longer have any appeal. Our ego will no longer guide our actions and covet what other men have. We MUST deal with the ego in order to overcome the lusts that draw us away from our relationship with Our Heavenly Father, our spouse, our children, and everyone we encounter.

TV commercials today are targeted to our ego. They promise us success, happiness, fitness, health, greater prowess, beauty, and the list goes on. We have been inundated with images and promises that suggest what we have is insufficient and we simply need to buy something else to bring us to a complete and fulfilled state. Most of this advertising is designed to encourage us to covet. We were all born with a void that needed to be filled but products, services, and exotic vacations will not fill that void. Only Love will fill the void and it begins with the relationship with Our Heavenly Father. As you grow closer to Our Heavenly Father, you will find that there is less appeal for "things" such as bigger houses, fancier cars, and the desire to be something you are not. Contentment replaces the cravings and you are no longer guided by the lust of the flesh, and the lust of the eyes, and the pride of life.

The third area of coveting has to do with your means of "making a living". The Tenth Commandment of Love mentions servants and livestock in the "do not covet" category. Financial success brings with it many trappings: houses, cars, prestige, etc. also known as the Great American Dream. All of this is temporary. The lure of coveting is a full-time endeavor and robs us of the focus we need to fulfill our own calling. As you focus on your own calling you will become disinterested in your neighbor's success and you clear the way for Our Heavenly Father to provide you with all the necessary tools you need to complete that which you have been called.

Your neighbor's success is based on his gifts and callings, not yours. Having traveled extensively on business, I can assure you that even the most beautiful sunset in Hawaii is just not that great without your loved one to share it with. Staying in an exclusive five star hotel without the love of your life is just another bed in an isolated room. Having one hundred fifty employees reporting to you seems exciting until the realities of the responsibility of them and their families are placed directly on your shoulders. Being stuck in an airport on Friday night when all your friends are enjoying dinner at the local restaurant is not to be envied.

Coveting always ends in emptiness. Our imaginations paint a picture of eternal bliss if we only had our neighbor's possessions. How many times have you bought something new to find out later that it did not fulfill what your imagination had promised? Isn't that the ploy of Madison Avenue advertising agencies to paint this picture of beauty, success, and fulfillment by just purchasing what is being advertised? Let's face it, clothes will not make us look like the model in the picture and a new car will not improve our status except as a borrower when we pay our loan on time.

Coveting is closely tied to consumption. If only we spent more money, took more vacations, hosted more parties, bought more clothes, our lives would be fulfilled. Wrong! Once the object of your imagination has been consumed, the emptiness and hunger return with a vengeance. Peace evades the person who has unbridled desires to lust after the things of this world.

Jesus was approached by a young rich man in search of the fulfillment we've been discussing:

Mat 19:16-24:

16 Now behold, one came and said to Him, "Good Teacher, what good thing shall I do that I may have eternal life?"

17 So He said to him, "Why do you call Me good? No one is good but One, that is, God. But if you want to enter into life, keep the commandments."

18 He said to Him, "Which ones?" Jesus said, "'You shall not murder,' 'You shall not commit adultery,' 'You shall not steal,' 'You shall not bear false witness,'

19 'Honor your father and your mother,' and, 'You shall love your neighbor as yourself.'"

20 The young man said to Him, "All these things I have kept from my youth. What do I still lack?"

21 Jesus said to him, "If you want to be perfect, go, sell what you have and give to the poor, and you will have treasure in heaven; and come, follow Me."

22 But when the young man heard that saying, he went away sorrowful, for he had great possessions.

23 Then Jesus said to His disciples, "Assuredly, I say to you that it is hard for a rich man to enter the kingdom of heaven.

24 "And again I say to you, it is easier for a camel to go through the eye of a needle than for a rich man to enter the kingdom of God."

Jesus shows us through the conversation with the rich young man that wealth does not fill that vacuum and the rich young man knew it by the mere fact he had wealth but wanted what Jesus was preaching- eternal life. This passage clearly shows us the challenge set before those with wealth. Jesus quoted six of the Ten Commandments to the young man who had claimed to have kept them from his youth. Was his wealth obtained from lawlessness connected with these commandments? Why would Jesus tie these commandments to the rich young man's wealth if there was not some connection to the source of the wealth which required the young man to be cleansed of the wealth in order to enter the kingdom of heaven?

Coveting is tied directly to the accumulation of wealth which in turn funds the lust of the flesh, the lust of the eyes, and the pride of life. Wealth in itself is not bad when it is used as a servant to your calling. Ill gotten gains must be cleansed and removed from you in order for you to be restored to Our Heavenly Father. If wealth has become your god, you are coveting. Let love cleanse you from this ego-centric lawlessness and restore you to Our Heavenly Father who can fill the void in your life with peace that passeth all understanding and it shall keep your heart and mind through Christ Jesus.

Chapter 4

LOVE DOES NOT BOAST

Self promotion results from the belief and insecurity that Our Heavenly Father is not truly in control and thus we need to promote ourselves to others. Excessive extolling oneself to others is boasting and often begins a sentence with "I" with frequent use of "me". Jesus was the Son of the Most High God and Possessor of the Universe. If anyone had "bragging rights" it was Jesus yet we read:

Philippians 2:7: But made himself of no reputation, and took upon him the form of a servant, and was made in the likeness of men.

This is critically important to understand: Jesus took on all the attributes of humanity and was subjected to all we are subjected to so that he could lawfully go to the cross as an innocent lamb and as an acceptable sacrifice. He knew his mission yet he did not put on a big marketing campaign to advertise his calling. He simply went about doing good. Our egos would have us do otherwise.

We are bombarded with encouragement toward self-promotion in books, the media, and in school. In grade school, my fifth grade teacher would have us challenge each other at the blackboard to see who could solve math problems quicker than the other. This competition always had a winner who could boast of a superior intellect. These little contests in life continually build a view that we must promote ourselves as being superior to others in order to get what we want out of life.

Each of us develops belief systems that result from us conforming to those who impact our lives. As a result of conditioning, we grow up developing a belief system consistent with our individual environment. However, this differs from our core beliefs that were placed there when we were formed in the womb. The core beliefs and characteristics can be suppressed but not eliminated because they lie at the center of the heart. What you truly believe comes from these core beliefs even though they are affected by who you think you are, what others tell you, and your responses to survival. Your survival may take place on the schoolyard, in the business world, or on the battlefield.

People want to be defined by external factors. Professional sports promote their popularity and revenue around the fans' desire to associate with winners. College football programs thrive as their teams win and provide their fans with boasting rights. How many people define their day based on whether their team wins or loses? The ego wants to claim superiority over others and sports provides an excellent venue to satisfy that craving. Oops! Did I attack another sacred cow?

Who we are is determined by what is in our hearts and what is in our hearts will promote us to our calling. As we mature, we begin to reflect about the mysteries of life and our part in those mysteries. There are four attributes to our calling: knowledge, skill, wisdom, and understanding. The crucial ingredient of our calling is wisdom:

Proverbs 4:5-6:

5 Get wisdom, get understanding: forget [it] not; neither decline from the words of my mouth.

6 Forsake her not, and she shall preserve thee: love her, and she shall keep thee.

7 Wisdom [is] the principal thing; [therefore] get wisdom: and with all thy getting get understanding.

8 Exalt her, and she shall promote thee: she shall bring thee to honour, when thou dost embrace her

Wisdom will promote your calling therefore you don't have to be your own marketing department. As you pursue your calling, Our Heavenly Father will do the promoting to others. HE will open the eyes of those who need to see your calling and they will embrace it for HE knows what tasks need to be accomplished and how those tasks will sustain you through this life.

Our Heavenly Father was speaking to Moses about building the Tabernacle in the wilderness. This was going to be a notable task to say the least. Every aspect of the Tabernacle was to tell a story that would span generations for this represented the epic relationship between GOD and man. Those that have studied the Tabernacle in the wilderness know that everything mentioned in Scripture had a specific meaning and was a type and shadow of the path to a fulfilling relationship with The Father. Who do you get to lead the building and construction program? Surely Moses was not prepared to build "world class" instruments needed in the Tabernacle. Who was prepared to take on this task at this point in history?

Exodus 31:1-5:

1 THEN the LORD spoke to Moses, saying:

2 "See, I have called by name Bezalel the son of Uri, the son of Hur, of the tribe of Judah.

3 "And I have filled him with the Spirit of God, in wisdom, in understanding, in knowledge, and in all manner of workmanship,

4 "to design artistic works, to work in gold, in silver, in bronze,

5 "in cutting jewels for setting, in carving wood, and to work in all manner of workmanship. (NKJV)

In Scripture, names and numbers are always relevant and their specific meanings and their use provides us a deeper understanding. Bezaleel means "in the shadow (i.e. protection) of God". When did Bezaleel's preparation for building the Tabernacle begin? It was the moment he was formed in the womb of his mother! Do you think his mother realized the magnitude of his calling when she gave birth to him? Bezaleel was one of those in bondage in Egypt and seemed destined to a life under the Egyptian yoke. "Then suddenly" Bezaleel was thrust out of Egypt freed from his harsh bondage and put in the wilderness by Jehovah seeing the pillar of smoke and fire by night. He was one of a couple of million people being led through the wilderness. Until it was time to build the Tabernacle, he was unknown to us. Who had the ability to build something satisfactory to the MOST HIGH GOD? It was this very man who Our Heavenly Father had prepared since he was formed in the womb. What a plan! It was Our Heavenly Father who would promote Bezaleel to be the head of the construction project. The Scripture provides the blueprint for the way life should be where each person and their gifts and callings are fitly joined together supplying the whole of civilization.

Love walks in humility. A humble person is a characteristically unpretentious and modest person who does not think that he or she is better or more important than others. A boastful person makes conscious efforts to direct attention to themselves usually at the expense of others. However we must be careful not to use these descriptions to judge others since the intent of this book is to provide a basis for each of us to look in the mirror and expose our own intents and purposes.

The Book of Proverbs frequently provides a contrast of opposites to give the reader a sense of what is right versus wrong or a sense of moral direction. The following is a great example:

Proverbs 18:12: Before destruction the heart of man is haughty, and before honour [is] humility. (KJV)

Being haughty, high-minded, or boastful moves a person toward destruction. As the popular saying goes, "His mouth is writing checks his body can't cash". We can train our brain to believe a lie if we continue to speak the lie long enough. How many times have you heard of a child who has been told that they will never amount to anything to the point they actually believe it? Words have power for Our Heavenly Father framed the world with words. We must guard our hearts from words that lead us astray from our purpose and calling and depart from those conversations and actions that would dilute our hearts and our minds. I have been guilty of boasting as I suspect most of us have. Our culture promotes boasting whether it physical, mental, economical, sexual, or social. How many times have I had to repent of my boastful actions and/or words! Those boastful words attempt to exalt you above the people around you resulting in a lord/servant positioning so that you exert some type of control over that person. It's all about subtle manipulation by the ego to exalt itself to a "god" status.

As you begin to understand Love you will start looking at others from a different perspective as well as yourself. Your sensitivity to boasting will begin to cut you short when the boasting begins. If you boast, you will immediately reflect on it and be convicted of it. This is when your heart takes charge over your ego. Don't get me wrong, you will have opportunities to speak about your gifts but the delivery will change from boasting to humility. With the revelation of Love, you will be able to look beyond the person who is boasting and see what is missing in their life and you may be called to fill it or at least address it in a loving way. When that man comes into the room with a loud voice and drawing attention to himself, you will now look at him with compassion. Our Heavenly Father may reveal to you that as a child he was beat incessantly and was locked out of the house by his foster parents as a form of child abuse. You will be able to look deep into his eyes and see his longing for a father's or mother's acceptance. You may be able to fill that void.

Boasting may be the result of the insecurity of a person's financial future. The person may feel compelled to constantly market his or her qualities in hope of a more secure future. Until the core belief that Our Heavenly Father will truly provide all our needs and desire according to His riches in glory, our insecurities about the future will surface and our ego will use that insecurity to rule over us.

As our inner man is strengthened, our tendency to boast about ourselves will diminish. As we continue to pursue a close Love relationship with Our Heavenly Father we will find ourselves maturing even though at times we may seem to be reverting back to our old ways. When we enter our prayer closet to confront the source of our boasting, Our Heavenly Father will tenderly begin to change us. With great grace and mercy HE will expose the source of the boasting and begin to do a progressive heart surgery and remove those sacred rooms where we never allowed anyone in. You know those rooms. They are the ones where you have built insurmountable walls around them to allow no one in. They may contain childhood rejections that you just could not understand. Other rooms may contain embarrassments from your school days. Some may contain business failures while others may contain failures as a parent.

Live life as an open book. Do not be afraid to admit your weaknesses to others. Know that Our Heavenly Father ultimately has your back. People yearn for honesty in their lives and those they associate with. Take a chance and let your friends know the real you because that person is who they are really drawn to. It may be painful at first but truth rewards those who pursue it.

Proverbs 3:3-4:
3 Let not mercy and truth forsake you;
Bind them around your neck,
Write them on the tablet of your heart,
4 And so find favor and high esteem
In the sight of God and man

Let Our Heavenly Father promote you, not your ego. As you do, you will find that the doors to your calling will open wide and you will enter into His rest.

Chapter 5

LOVE IS NOT PUFFED UP

"Puffed up" means to be proud in a lofty sense. In today's use, the term "proud" can mean: feeling self-respect or pleasure in something by which you measure your self-worth. However, when your ego elevates that measurement to an exalted status, you are puffed up.

It is important to feel worthy. Our Heavenly Father, the Possessor of Heaven and earth saw fit to create you and place you on this earth to carry out a purpose He intended for you to complete. That is important and worthy of your consideration. He is the potter and you are the clay and He molded you into His creation. You are not an accident! On the other hand, be careful to understand your calling of "service".

We have all heard the cliché credited to Lord Acton in 1887 "Power corrupts and absolute power corrupts absolutely". This quotation still applies today as we observe political leaders rise to power. In the U.S. leaders call themselves "public servants" yet generally acts like kings and queens. It does not take long for a person to listen to accolades about his accomplishments, his intelligence, or any other exceptional quality before he becomes puffed up and arrogant.

The Book of Psalms speaks frequently of "the proud" which tells us that this facet of the ego must be dealt with in no uncertain terms.

Psalms 119:78: Let the proud be ashamed; for they dealt perversely with me without a cause: [but] I will meditate in thy precepts. (KJV)

One of the subtleties of this Scripture is that the proud will subvert the law and deal perversely with the righteous. They will falsify information in order to maintain their lofty status. When mans exalts himself, much energy is required to maintain this false status and at some point the energy will subside only to reveal the true nature of the individual. I once worked with a man who wrote all of his business conversations down on paper in order to remember what he said to each person he spoke to. Why not rely on the truth? This man was in a position of authority and was a master manipulator but his days were numbered. Ultimately, the business failed. His technical prowess elevated him to a partner in the business only to find he was not equipped to manage people. In business circles this phenomenon is known as "The Peter Principle".

Another aspect of this Scripture is the "without a cause" characteristic. This is slander, pure and simple. Slander or defamation is defined as words falsely spoken that damage the reputation of another. When you speak falsely of another, you place yourself as an adversary of Our Heavenly Father. Your lawlessness opens the door to judgments which can take the form of sickness, disease, eroding relationships, job loss, or other disastrous events. There is a fine line between accurately reporting the actions of another and adding your own interpretation of their intent. We must be careful to speak the truth and present facts accurately. Our Heavenly Father will not necessarily execute judgment in the same arena as your lawlessness and time delay is not a limiting factor to these judgments.

People have been taught that sickness and disease is from the devil. The question that begs to be asked is "Who writes the devil's paycheck"? Our Heavenly Father! He created the devil and knew the purpose of each and every being HE created. Are you not convinced? Read the following from Deuteronomy:

Deuteronomy 32:23-24,39:
23 'I will heap disasters on them;
I will spend My arrows on them.
24 They shall be wasted with hunger,
Devoured by pestilence and bitter destruction;
I will also send against them the teeth of beasts,
With the poison of serpents of the dust.
39 'Now see that I, even I, am He,
And there is no God besides Me;
I kill and I make alive;
I wound and I heal;
Nor is there any who can deliver from My hand.

ALL power in Heaven and earth is The Lord's, no exceptions. When you are prideful and move away from a servant's heart, you open the door to judgments. If left unchecked, the pendulum swings to the extreme and so does the correction. Think about it.

Proverbs 16:18 Pride [goeth] before destruction, and an haughty spirit before a fall. (KJV)

Arrogance or haughty spirit places you in a position to lose the very thing you are arrogant about. Being puffed up like a balloon puts you in a room full of needles where the issue is not "if" but "when". This puffed up behavior will entrap you in a progressive manner and before you know it, you have suffered a fall. Who determines the severity of that fall? Our Heavenly Father does through His righteous judgments knowing all of the particulars of your life and the appropriate judgment to teach you a lesson.

Most of us have experienced the corrections I'm mentioning. When I was a young businessman I worked for a company where I became the fair haired boy and was promoted to a position of management. I worked hard and was rewarded for that. My influence increased and so did the size of my ego. I went to church, exercised my faith, and wore my Christian "badge of honor". Then suddenly I came down with hepatitis after I ingested shellfish at a New York meeting. Though in the previous five years I had never been off work due to sickness, I came down with "the big one". I had a severe case and the doctor expressed grave concern.

He told me to expect to be off work for six to eight weeks. Unbelievable! I asked Our Heavenly Father how this could happen to me and HE said "You are void of My Word". As any puffed up person would do, I argued with Him. I had consistently studied Scripture, listened to teaching tapes, and read Christian books about faith and other subjects. He asked, "When was the last time you studied My Word on healing?" I sadly replied "It's been a while", and I repented. In His great grace and mercy, he healed me and I was back to work in eleven days. My balloon had been popped.

Being puffed up has at its source a view of independence. When we start believing that our successes are attributed purely to our own ability without any intervention from Our Heavenly Father, we are in deep trouble. Lack of perspective contributes to that path of destruction. Our personal experiences are woefully insufficient to grasp the big picture. An excellent example of this is found in the Book of Esther. The king had a lawless queen who needed to be replaced. Esther was chosen. Her uncle Mordecai had counseled her in her preparation to be chosen. Unknown to the king, Mordecai foils a plot to assassinate the king and it is recorded in the daily chronicles. Haman comes onto the scene and is promoted by the king to an important staff position above the others in the king's government. The subjects of the kingdom are to bow down to Haman and now Haman is in the "puffed up" stage. However, Mordecai does not bow down to Haman. We see the plot thicken as Haman becomes furious with Mordecai's insubordination. Haman devises a plan to kill Mordecai. Before he can carry out the plan, something unexpected happens. One night, the king cannot sleep and asks that the daily chronicles be read to him and he heard of Mordecai's deed to foil the assassination attempt. The king wanted to reward Mordecai to a position of honor. Who was to carry this out? Haman. Ultimately, the gallows Haman had built to hang Mordecai was used on himself.

Haman's fortune turned when the king could not sleep. Was it a coincidence? Had Haman known of the event, he could have been saved. His limited perspective of the big picture did not allow him that privilege. Our Heavenly Father is the only one who has full knowledge of all the interactions in the universe. When our complete trust is placed in Him, we have the advantage of knowing that all things work together for our good as He directs our footsteps. Once we move away to a point of independence, our pride and ego steps with an attempt to exalt us to a "god" status and that is where destruction begins.

The Apostle Paul warns us about those who would use deceptive methods to convince us of another doctrine other than Gospel of Christ.

Colossians 2:18: Do not let anyone who delights in false humility and the worship of angels disqualify you for the prize. Such a person goes into great detail about what he has seen, and his unspiritual mind puffs him up with idle notions. (NIV)

In this verse, the person claims to see a vision or revelation and expects to be exalted to a prominent status because of that event. It is a real challenge to us to refrain from exalting ourselves when we participate in a "spiritual" event. Let's say for instance that Our Heavenly Father has you to lay hands on the sick and they recover. Let's assume the sickness is stage 4 cancer and they have only weeks to live. You do as you are instructed and the cancer shrivels up and goes away. Who was the source of the healing? You? Our egos would have us to believe that once that event occurs, we have now been endowed with a new power. We start getting calls from those who heard about the miracle. They want to receive some of this healing power too. Can we muster up another miracle?

We are told by Our Heavenly Father not to worship the created, only the Creator. We are to have no other gods before Him. When we exalt another person's gifts or calling, we are redirecting our worship to them. Compliments are not forms of worship but obsessive behavior focused on another person, animal, place, or thing is. We are all internally wired to worship someone or some thing. Some people worship wealthy people, others worship athletes. Some worship their pets and there are those that even worship statues. We must consider both sides of being "puffed up".

Being puffed up also connects itself with judgment. Once your ego has exalted to you a higher status relative to others in your sphere of influence, you anoint yourself judge. What a tangled web our ego weaves. Unrighteous judgment is a favorite plot of television drama. We all cheer for the victim of this judgment who is vindicated when the self righteous villain is brought to justice.

Are you puffed up? Do you constantly promote yourself

at the expense of others? Think about the people who once wanted to be close to you who are now gone out of your life. Why? What circumstances caused them to drift away from you? Pure love attracts!

Chapter 6

LOVE DOES NOT BEHAVE RUDELY

*L*ove is not disrespectful and does not act unbecomingly. Disrespect belittles the other person which once again exalts oneself as being superior. Personal attacks on others are designed to create an enemy which in turn creates a justification for further rude behavior. The Apostle Paul writes:

Romans 13:7 Give everyone what you owe him: If you owe taxes, pay taxes; if revenue, then revenue; if respect, then respect; if honour, then honour. (NIV)

Our rude actions and responses are usually designed to get things "our way". If you won't agree to my agenda, I will punish you with my rude actions. Rude behavior has at its source, manipulation.

Sixteen years ago I was in the middle of a business contract issue. The other party wanted me to put together terms and conditions of a contract on an asset purchase. It was my custom to pray an hour each morning before I started the business day. I was asking The Father about the contract and He said "Do nothing". I asked why? He said, "When you negotiate, you manipulate, and manipulation is not of Me!" What an impact it had on me! I viewed myself as a shrewd negotiator and was now convicted of my sin. What did I do? Nothing. Two weeks passed and the other party asked me where my agreement was at. I responded that I did not have one and he pulled one out which far exceeded my expectations. I could not have negotiated a better deal.

When we are young, we try out rude behavior in an effort to get our own way. Generally our parents nip that behavior in the bud. However if there is any success at all, our little brains file it away in our toolkit to use at a later time. As time goes by, we develop rude behavior as a protection mechanism as well as a manipulative method to further our agenda.

Behind rude behavior often we find insecurity. Insecurity is the anxiety you experience when you feel vulnerable and vulnerability prevails when you do not have a solid relationship with Our Heavenly Father. He knows your every need and will direct you through and around adversity. Without this relationship, you feel vulnerable to the storms of life and feel you must protect yourself and become skeptical in your relationship with others. You then place a shell around your heart to protect it from any pain or suffering that others might inflict on it. This protection mode then moves toward rude behavior. This shell may be a result of a failed relationship where you opened up your heart and was intimate with your most inner feelings only to have the other person take advantage of you in your vulnerable state. Young men have often been the perpetrators of this offence against vulnerable women who long for a mate to share their life and their love. This unbecoming behavior by men has left its scar on countless women who then put up barriers around themselves and are unwilling to let those with pure intentions into their lives. It then starts a vicious cycle.

"I'll show you who is boss." That attitude is projected by cutting someone off in traffic, giving a waiter in a restaurant a hard time, or expressing anger at an airport gate attendant because your plane in late. This rude behavior targets the innocent and unsuspecting. Why do I act so rude? Am I feeling guilty about something I've done and I simply redirect the guilt to the next person I come in contact with?

Instead of acting rudely, we should be courteous to every person we encounter. The problem with that rule is that unless we are at peace with Our Heavenly Father and ourselves, that will not happen. It is like that New Year's resolution, we start out with good intentions but soon the emotion of the commitment was worn off. What is in our heart ultimately guides our footsteps and our actions. If we have turmoil in our heart, we will create turmoil in our encounters with others. If we have peace in our hearts, we will spread peace to those we meet. Our guilt of sin will somehow punish each person we encounter whether in traffic, at a restaurant, or in our home.

In a practical sense, there is no value to acting rudely. You alienate the other person targeted by your rudeness and damage the relationship even if it only a temporary encounter. When you reject the other person, you are rejecting their gifts and calling and the opportunity to be blessed by them. Let wisdom prevail in your life instead:

Psalms 101:2: I will behave wisely in a perfect way. Oh, when will You come to me? I will walk within my house with a perfect heart. (NKJV)

At our core, we want to be accepted by other people. At an early age we want to please our parents, grandparents, and any other important people in our lives. This need of acceptance is strong in all of us. Only by consistent rejection do we build a wall of protection around our hearts to defend ourselves against this rejection. If the wall becomes too high, our ability to accept others may be impossible to achieve. We dish out the same rejection we received during our formative years thus creating a "generational curse". Our Heavenly Father has the means to not only scale that wall but to dismantle it as well. Our ego uses the knowledge of someone's strong need of acceptance as a means to control that other person. It is often seen in a mother/daughter relationship. The mother grew up in a home where her need to be accepted was not satisfied and thus she never knew what a fulfilling relationship was like. Once she had her own daughter, she simply repeated the process robbing her daughter of the "blessing" of a close giving relationship with her mother. What a shame! Over the years, I have seen countless examples of this situation in mother/daughter relations. Many daughters have cried in their pillows because of the failure of their mothers to simply accept them, love them, and enjoy a relationship with them.

With sons the wall creates a response of insensitivity. Bitterness and anger are often the outworking of a son who could never receive acceptance. Sometimes the son will seek to perform in such a fashion as to prove the parent wrong using the "I'll show you" attitude. Other times, the son may simply give up and believe the rejection to be the reality of his life and underachieve in everything. What a vicious cycle the ego can create when allowed to rule the person's life!

Fortunately, Our Heavenly Father's love can scale any wall of protection built by the ego. The rude behavior is simply a symptom of a deeper issue. The Holy Spirit can soften even the toughest and the strongest. There is nothing that is locked up in the deepest recesses of the heart that cannot be exposed and dealt with. Why hold on to that hurt any longer? Why let someone else dictate how your day will be spent? Why let someone else's turmoil determine your peace or lack thereof? You are accepted by your Heavenly Father for He is fully responsible for bringing you forth into this world, at this time, and with your specific parents. If you can grasp that revelation, your life will change immediately for the better. Your earthly parents were conduits for your arrival on earth but they do not hold the autonomous power over you unless you grant them the power as a surrogate. You are a child of GOD and have the rights and privileges associated with that reality. Even though your earthly parents may have failed to nurture you, love you, accept you, and support you; your inheritance as a child of GOD is awaiting your revelation. Your Heavenly Father will never leave you or forsake you but will guide you toward your gifts and calling in Love. Those walls you built for protection will tumble down just like the walls of Jericho. Instead of constantly apologizing for something you didn't do and then taking the mantle of rudeness from your parent, you will become the loving, caring person that people will be attracted to. Accept Love as the basis of your relationships, not rejection.

Acts of rudeness must be cast aside in order for you to fulfill your calling. Alienation of others will slow your progress toward maturity. Responding to rudeness with rudeness will not break the cycle but instead walk in Love. Love will ultimately convict the other person who has found safety under the cloak of rudeness. Once you understand the rudeness is a symptom of the root of bitterness, you will be able to minister to the other person. Revelation elevates your understanding and pulls you out of the level that the other person is operating in. Once you are elevated above the problem, ministry of restoration can begin. However, if you fail to seek out the revelation of the problem, you will continue to be subject to the problem and receive the harsh rewards of an unfriendly taskmaster.

Throughout this writing, you can see that the ego has waged a war against the revelation of Love. With its "take no prisoners" attitude, the ego is fighting for supremacy. It is the "goat" symbol in Scripture. There were two goat sacrifices: one to be sacrificed at the mercy seat, the other to be led out into the Wilderness by a "fit" man. (Leviticus 16) These goats were part of a sin offering. The root word for "goat" means: to storm, shiver, dread, bristle (with horror), be very afraid; to storm away, sweep away, whirl away. The devil's symbol has been described as a goat head. This symbolism is indicative of the actions of the ego. The ego is self-centered whereas Love is self-sacrificing. The ego wants to be lord over others whereas Love serves others. Your ego must be sacrificed at the Mercy Seat of Our Heavenly Father. In addition, your ego must be led into the wilderness by a "fit" man to be removed from the people thus indicating that you should no longer live by your ego but distance yourself from its influence. Just as Jesus fulfilled the "goat" sacrifice by being led into the wilderness for a time of testing, we all must be tested as well. When the devil came to tempt Jesus, the devil tried to use the ego as the means of drawing Jesus away from His calling. Love prevailed and Jesus was not overcome by the temptations. The "fit" man symbolized the Holy Spirit and Jesus walked in the revelation of Love and knew by His Father's words that there was no power on earth that could stand against Love. His example should be our encouragement that we do not need to use the instruments of the ego to manipulate and hurt others with rude behavior. On the contrary, as we walk in Love, the walls of bitterness and insecurity will come tumbling down revealing the pure hearts of acceptance and Love that were created by Our Heavenly Father.

Chapter 7

LOVE IS NOT SELF SERVING

*L*ove does not "seeketh after her own" or in other words, Love is not selfish. In habitually placing your own needs and desires above others you will never learn how to serve mankind. Selfishness promotes the belief of scarcity and the inability of Our Heavenly Father to meet our every need.

In the first years of my life, I was the center of the universe. My mother fed me when I was hungry, changed my diaper when it was soiled, and comforted me when I cried. Life was simple and seemed pretty complete at the time. As I grew older, the center of the universe no longer revolved around me. Our family structure required service such as mowing the lawn, picking up my room, and helping with the dishes after dinner. I was expected to serve the family structure. Attempts to continue with my self serving attitude were met by that disciplining "look" of my dad. His look spoke volumes and I understood the law of the land and the ramifications of breaking that law.

When I was young I tended to be selfish and self serving. It seemed that if I wanted to move forward in life, I needed to do it myself and no one was going to help me get there. I worked in the family business and made seventeen cents per hour. Even though I had friends with less, my wages were insufficient to really buy much of anything. On top of that, my dad forced me to save 25% of my wages. What a slave driver! I wanted more so I asked for a raise to twenty-five cents per hour and after much pain, it was granted. I knew what scarcity was at a young age and believed in it. I had no idea that Our Heavenly Father could or would bless me under any circumstances and so I was taught that the only way to get ahead was to "work hard and save your money". Don't get me wrong, working hard and saving your money is a noble path to take except that if you fail to understand serving and giving, you become self serving.

Self serving creates an attitude of irresponsibility concerning your gifts and calling. Without understanding the big picture, you assume your gifts are simply for self promotion. Everything revolves around you and your survival, promotion, and fulfillment. You look at relationships in light of what the other person can do for you, not what you can do for him or her. With this attitude, your calling suffers. Your calling is not to be hid under a bush but to be a light unto the world. As you focus inward instead of outward, your gifts and calling suffer due to the inhibiting force that will not allow your gifts to move you toward the fullness of a relationship with Our Heavenly Father. I am convinced that when you focus your gifts inward in a self serving fashion, Our Heavenly Father will not allow the fullness of blessing to occur. Why would any parent send the child the signals to reinforce the wrong path or action?

In the Book of Job, Our Heavenly Father made it quite clear to Job that there was a bigger picture that Job did not understand. Job's life had been turned upside down and he could not understand why bad things were happening to good people... or him! After much intellectual discussion with his friends, Our Heavenly Father shows up and shares with him the bigger picture. There are laws we do not understand or even have an awareness of. These laws have to do with the oneness of the universe. Our limited minds cannot understand the omnipresence of GOD. In our limitations we cannot understand how Our Heavenly Father can be everywhere at once. It is a mystery that our limited mental ability cannot grasp thus we cannot understand how something five thousand miles away can affect us. How can our prayer for someone in another country be of any value? Our self-centeredness limits our understanding and ultimately our impact on the rest of mankind.

We all serve someone or something, without exception. When we are in survival mode, we are serving our physical needs. In order to survive we will do whatever it takes to sustain life. When I was a baby, I did not hesitate to cry when I was hungry and when I was cold, I cried. Our survival instincts kick in immediately upon birth and are exercised frequently in our first years. We learn how to survive in the environment we are placed in. As our mind develops and our awareness expands, we begin to mentally serve ourselves. This phase may continue for the rest of your life if your awareness no longer expands beyond "self". People may hide their self serving orientation by using their social skills but nevertheless they still serve soul: me, myself, and I.

Only when one's awareness increases to a spiritual level does a new orientation of service occur. Once we realize that a Supreme Being created us and will have a relationship with us do we focus our attention on others at the sacrifice of self. This is when Love shows up on the radar. It may come at any age and does not require mental maturity to occur. Actually, strong and mentally advanced people tend to have difficulty in perceiving the spiritual realm because their mental faculties have served them well in not only promoting their survival but meeting all of their physical needs. The structure they created and surrounded themselves with is a surrogate to peace and takes a tremendous amount of energy and resource to keep it in place. At the center of their being is a void that needs filled and they will work and scheme to fill it with worldly desires, without success. That drive when taken to an extreme can consume the individual.

Mental acuteness promotes service to structure and structure promotes slavery. Structure will enslave you and demands you to serve and perpetuate it. There is an old saying, "It is easier to obtain than it is to maintain". When we accumulate possessions, the initial cost is only the beginning of the expense of having that possession. We must manage it, fix it, restore it, wear it out, and then finally dispose of it. How many times have you become a slave to a possession? Our family once bought a ski boat because we enjoyed water sports and our neighbor had taken us to the lake to go water skiing. We had a great time with fond memories and wanted to duplicate those memories. I bought a boat, stored it in the garage (taking the space of my car), and took it to the lake about five times a year. After two years and a couple of tune ups on the motor, I realized that the boat was a money pit and I was its slave. It would have been cheaper to rent a ski rig at the lake and walk away at the end of the weekend. I was attempting to serve a remembrance with structure and missed the point that it was the fellowship that brought the cherished memories, not the boat.

Structure promotes complexity and complexity promotes hierarchy. What is a hierarchy? A hierarchy is an arrangement of people according to a ranking of importance. What is wrong with creating a hierarchy? This is where judgment creeps in and you naturally place yourself at the top of the list of importance. Once you do this, you promote the self serving attitude and expect everyone to serve you. Hierarchies create an elitist attitude and this has become predominant in the thinking of Americans versus the rest of the world. With America's dominance in the economic and military arenas, many Americans believe that they have some sort of entitlement as being the elite of the world. Wealthy people tend to develop this elitist attitude by equating godliness with their wealth. They mistakenly assume that they have been specially "anointed" by Our Heavenly Father since they have been able to amass substantial wealth. Little do they realize that in Scripture, Our Heavenly Father would utilize the services of heathen kings to hold on to His property until the ordained time of Israel's captivity was completed. The classic Scripture revealing this is found in Isaiah:

Isaiah 45:1-3:

1 Thus saith the LORD to his anointed, to Cyrus, whose right hand I have holden, to subdue nations before him; and I will loose the loins of kings, to open before him the two leaved gates; and the gates shall not be shut;

2 I will go before thee, and make the crooked places straight: I will break in pieces the gates of brass, and cut in sunder the bars of iron:

3 And I will give thee the treasures of darkness, and hidden riches of secret places, that thou mayest know that I, the LORD, which call [thee] by thy name, [am] the God of Israel. (KJV)

Notice that Cyrus the king of Persia and conqueror of Babylon was called the "LORD'S anointed". Our Heavenly Father will use whomever he will to steward over wealth until the time HE needs to distribute it.

Hierarchical orientation is a worldly view, not a Heavenly view. People high up in the hierarchy perpetuate their relative position with a quest to move higher in the pecking order. "Survival of the fittest" is an elitist, self-serving view of the world. People are attempting to ascend to higher levels in their mind through layers of structured perception and promote that pathway to others in an attempt to control and dominate. Once again it is the haves versus the have not's. Once you have realized that you no longer belong to structure, you will be able to ascend to a higher relationship of love with mankind as well as Our Heavenly Father. As long as you maintain the illusion of structure being the sum of reality, you will be held captive to structure, hierarchy, and the current system of enslavement. Jesus proclaimed:

Luke 4:17-21:

17 And there was delivered unto him the book of the prophet Esaias. And when he had opened the book, he found the place where it was written,

18 The Spirit of the Lord [is] upon me, because he hath anointed me to preach the gospel to the poor; he hath sent me to heal the brokenhearted, to preach deliverance to the captives, and recovering of sight to the blind, to set at liberty them that are bruised,

19 To preach the acceptable year of the Lord.

20 And he closed the book, and he gave [it] again to the minister, and sat down. And the eyes of all them that were in the synagogue were fastened on him.

21 And he began to say unto them, This day is this scripture fulfilled in your ears. (KJV)

Jesus did not submit himself to man's structure yet He operated within it during His ministry. Isaiah had prophesied of Jesus in Chapter 61 and Jesus confirmed it in the above passage.

What is meant "to preach the gospel to the poor"? In Isaiah the verse references "meek" and both words are used in the Sermon on the Mount. I am convinced that the word "poor" represents the simple and uncomplicated people who are able to receive the simplicity of the Gospel without man's self serving interpretations to establish a hierarchy. Could it be that Jesus was sent to set us free of man's societal structures created to hold us captive within their system of values?

Broken hearts must be healed with Love and the message of the Gospel was to reassert Love has the foremost way of life. Dominance by carnal methods is no longer acceptable or tolerated by Heaven. Those blinded by fear and greed will see the error of their ways by the light of Love and those bruised by domineering, self-serving task master will be healed by the revelation of Love. The era of self-serving leadership and individuals is ending and the captivity of the poor is being dealt with by Our Heavenly Father. The move is on and the acceptable year of the Lord is at hand!

Chapter 8

LOVE IS NOT EASILY PROVOKED

*L*ove is not easily provoked to anger. Anger is a sensitive topic when discussing Love. Many of us have been led to believe that if you love someone, it is wrong to get angry but yet Our Heavenly Father was angered many times in Scripture. Anger precedes a righteous response of remedy otherwise you will sin. When confronted with sin, Our Heavenly Father's wrath or anger was a response of righteous judgment against the sins of the people.

Are you easily irritated? When we are not at peace within ourselves, we tend to project that state towards others as a justification for our lack of peace. Have you ever noticed when you have sinned within your heart and unknown to others, you find opportunities to be irritated at their behavior? It just seems that you are looking for a fight or a confrontation. This irritability usually has sin at its source. This sin may be from an action as well as inaction. Acts of sins are often easily revealed and dealt with but sins of inaction are subtle and may fester for years. Allowing yourself to be manipulated by another is not Our Heavenly Father's perfect will and some people will allow themselves to be miserable for years because they may be wanting or longing for acceptance from the manipulator but that day never comes. Only Love will fill that void.

We are told to not let the sun set on our anger:

Ephesians 4:26: Be ye angry, and sin not: let not the sun go down upon your wrath. (KVJ)

Anger is a "call to action". Your pulse increases and your breathing increases in preparation for action to remediate, to defend and protect the truth. The key is to sin not when responding to this call to action. Our Heavenly Father responded in righteous anger toward the sinfulness of the people. Anger heats things up. Purging sin requires a refiner's fire to separate the dross and purify our souls.

When I was a child my parents would tolerate some rebellion in my behavior. I knew the rules but from time to time I would test the limits, more so with my mother who was the "nurturer" rather than my dad who was the "enforcer". My young ego wanted to check out my ability to take control of the situation and find out just where that edge of the abyss was. My nurturing mother would allow me greater latitude when I was checking out the boundaries set for my protection. However, when I stepped over the line, my dad the enforcer arrived with swift and painful punishment. Did that mean they did not love me? On the contrary! They knew it was necessary to impress me with those boundaries of safety to protect me from certain danger. Their anger was to prevent danger.

Anger is a response to something that is contrary to righteous behavior:

Proverbs11:23: The desire of the righteous [is] only good: [but] the expectation of the wicked [is] wrath. (KJV)

The wicked know that wrath or anger will come because they provoke that response of judgment against them. Have you noticed how wicked people perpetuate the wrath of the Law and ultimately end up in prison or the grave?

We are told to be slow to anger so that we may fully understand the situation before taking action. For those of us with sons, how often have we looked for a tool and blamed our son for taking it only to find it near the last project we used it on? Our lack of complete understanding and information should warn us of moving to quick to judge a situation. Love will slow that process and allow for the possibility of another reason for an action by the other person.

Titus 1:15: Unto the pure all things [are] pure: but unto them that are defiled and unbelieving [is] nothing pure; but even their mind and conscience is defiled. (KJV)

This Scripture is an indictment against all of us who have misjudged a situation and accused the innocent. This passage provides us a litmus test to see where we really stand in our hearts. Have you become cynical toward others? Are you always looking for the angle in someone's interaction with you? Do you ask yourself "What is it that they are after?" "What is their motive?" You must check your heart because your impurities are causing you to view others with cynicism and defensiveness. These impurities will provoke a response before one is necessary and will in many cases cause division between you and the other person.

It is critical to take an inward view of yourself when you have been provoked to anger by another. You must answer the question of whether your anger resulted from their unrighteous actions or your deep seeded guilt surfacing as a defense mechanism. Did you trap the other person into a situation where you could evoke your wrath on them? Is their behavior generally irritating you and so you start looking for a reason for confrontation? This is not Love. Love looks to correct and redeem the other person, not attack them.

Love is not wimpy even though it has been stereotyped to be passive and weak at times. Jesus is our example of complete and unconditional Love. The Scriptural accounts of Matthew, Mark, and Luke show us another facet of Love. Here is the account of Mark:

Mark 11:15-18:

15 And they come to Jerusalem: and Jesus went into the temple, and began to cast out them that sold and bought in the temple, and overthrew the tables of the moneychangers, and the seats of them that sold doves;

16 And would not suffer that any man should carry [any] vessel through the temple.

17 And he taught, saying unto them, Is it not written,

My house shall be called of all nations the house of prayer? but ye have made it a den of thieves.

18 And the scribes and chief priests heard [it], and sought how they might destroy him: for they feared him, because all the people was astonished at his doctrine.

From the above passage we see that sin fears Love, not the reverse. The moneychangers had defiled the temple and had commercialized it. Jesus single handedly drove them out of the temple and astonished the people. Love is not just a passive emotion cowering down to dominating, socially accepted rebellious people. Love hears Our Heavenly Father's voice and acts accordingly. Jesus did not appear as a weakling to the moneychangers but was empowered by Love and acted on the words of His Father who is also our Father as well. Our Heavenly Father saw fit to give a triple witness of this facet which demands our full attention to this aspect of Love.

Love does not start wars, it ends them. Israel was expecting a conquering messiah but instead Jesus came to save the world through Love and went to the cross. Israel was blinded by their doctrine to the point that the Son of God walked among them and they could not "see" Him for who He was. Today many people are looking for that same messiah to come down and evoke a global judgment and throw all those sinners into a lake of fire forever. "That will show them"! Do you think that Our Heavenly Father who opens eyes and closes eyes, opens ears and closes ears, will really send people to burn for eternity? If GOD IS LOVE and

Love is not easily provoked, there must be another level of understanding about those Scriptures that have led many to believe the "turn or burn" doctrine.

The Law in Scripture represents the character of the Lawgiver and there was no punishment that compared to the "burning in hell" doctrine. We must either believe that Our Heavenly Father has a perfect plan of redemption or HE failed to account for all soulish actions of His creation. Jesus' actions were not conditional to whether you or I agreed to be righteous and committed to serve mankind. There was no if, then. Clearly, the patience of Our Heavenly Father supersedes His wrath or this whole world would have been wiped out long ago. The Creator is ultimately accountable for the created!

Paul writes:

Colossians 3:21: Fathers, provoke not your children [to anger], lest they be discouraged.

If by the Holy Spirit, Paul wrote the above passage, how could Our Heavenly Father promote anger among His children? Anger is a temporary event to remediate a situation that requires immediate action.

Sustained anger brings forth bitterness which in turn hinders your ability to have an intimate relationship with Our Heavenly Father. To reiterate, the source of this anger is at the root of bitterness and will adversely impact your all of your relationships:

Hebrews 12:14-15:

14 Pursue peace with all people, and holiness, without which no one will see the Lord:

15 looking carefully lest anyone fall short of the grace of God; lest any root of bitterness springing up cause trouble, and by this many become defiled; (KJV)

That bitterness may be towards a parent, specifically your father. It seems that many earthly fathers are guilty of failing to provide a holy and righteous example to their children. In turn, the damage done to these children reverberates throughout society with those that are closest to the suffering children receive the brunt of the fallout. The pent up anger in these children creates protective walls and they become chameleons when among a group of people. They will attempt to be all things to all people thus losing their true identity. This may go on for decades and adversely affect the lives of their spouses and children. The sin continues from generation to generation. Love will break the cycle as we come to terms with the sin and expose it to light. Children have painted the face of their earthly father on Our Heavenly Father resulting in the inability to have a close and intimate relationship with Our Heavenly Father. Once that anger has been dealt with and the root of bitterness has been plucked up, the close relationship longed for will emerge. No longer will people have to tolerate or avoid the person with anger issues and relationships will be mended. Joy will come forth and the radiance of Love will replace the darkness of bitterness. Those years of anxiety and regret will fade away to a distant memory.

As we walk in Love, we will give no place for bitterness to root and we will no longer be known for our quick temper or our tendency to lash out at others. We will no longer be easily provoked.

Chapter 9

LOVE THINKS NO EVIL

*T*he word "evil" occurs 613 times in the King James Version of the Bible. It just happens that the total number of commandments and statutes acknowledged by the Jews are 613. Hmmm! The word "evil" means troublesome, injurious, destructive, wicked, or of a bad nature. Man's nature wants to judge others, usually for gain or recognition, thus exalting the ego and lifting himself high above those around him. The ego's goal is supremacy at the expense of anyone who would get in the way. I once heard a speaker give a contrasting definition of Love- "Love is the sacrifice of self for the benefit of others, lust is the sacrifice of others for the benefit of self". This simple comparison provides a test of whether your actions fall into the category of Love or the fulfillment of the ego.

Often we misconstrue thought as the culprit in the phrase "as a man thinks, so is he". A better translation of that phrase would be "as a man intends, so is he". Thought is not the culprit but intent is! A thought about evil is not the issue because we are bombarded with evil daily and simply thinking about evil in the world is not sin. But to dwell on evil and developing intent is the issue. Men are visual animals and that is why women spend billions of dollars every year on makeup, clothes, and hair products to get the attention of men. The media understands what draws men's attention and they exploit that core tendency by using "sex" in their advertising directed towards men.

Jesus spoke the following:

Matthew 5:27-28:

27 "You have heard that it was said to those of old, 'You shall not commit adultery.'

28 "But I say to you that whoever looks at a woman to lust for her has already committed adultery with her in his heart. (NKJV)

Jesus warns us that intent is where the issue lies. In the Old Testament, the laws were designed to prevent the action of sin, that is, to modify the behavior of people. However, when Jesus dealt with this topic in the above Scripture, He revealed to us that the sin occurred before the action. We cannot eliminate people and things that can be lusted after for the change must occur in our hearts. Thoughts are not evil but dwelling on evil ultimately moves us toward intent. As we dwell on lust or evil, we begin to build a plan in our mind to carry out the act. But our ego will play a game with us. In normal thought processes we consider all alternatives before we take action as a defense against failure. If you were considering buying a new car, you might think about the cost of acquisition, the potential maintenance costs, the monthly obligation and how it might affect your ability to purchase other necessities. Once you have played the scenarios out, you then decide to purchase the vehicle. Now I understand there are those who take a more emotional approach and simply buy the car, but the person who ponders the purchase will most likely have no regrets.

When the ego impacts the thought process, something happens. The negatives of an evil thought are suppressed and not considered as an alternative action so the planned action is flawed once you begin to run through the various scenarios. Our spirit must override the ego's attempt to deceive us in believing an illusion. There is a truism, "You become like the company you keep" and as we continually expose ourselves to right thinking we will gain control of those thoughts that move us to sin. The following passage exhorts to do so:

Philippians 4:8: Finally, brethren, whatsoever things are true, whatsoever things [are] honest, whatsoever things [are] just, whatsoever things [are] pure, whatsoever things [are] lovely, whatsoever things [are] of good report; if [there be] any virtue, and if [there be] any praise, think on these things. (KJV)

Love unites whereas evil divides. When Jesus healed a demon-possessed, blind and mute man, he was challenged by the Pharisees. They tried to assign His power to Beelzebub but knowing their evil thoughts, He told us that every kingdom divided against itself would fall. Rather than be overjoyed by the healing of this man, their authority was challenged and they were more concerned about their status than the miracle that just occurred. How blinded we become by our ego! During this confrontation, Jesus shares a truth about how we can determine what is in a person's heart—Listen to his words.

Mat 12:33-37:

33 "Either make the tree good and its fruit good, or else make the tree bad and its fruit bad; for a tree is known by its fruit.

34 "Brood of vipers! How can you, being evil, speak good things? For out of the abundance of the heart the mouth speaks.

35 "A good man out of the good treasure of his heart[fn7] brings forth good things, and an evil man out of the evil treasure brings forth evil things.

36 "But I say to you that for every idle word men may speak, they will give account of it in the day of judgment.

37 "For by your words you will be justified, and by your words you will be condemned." (NKJV)

As we dwell on evil, those thoughts become "abundant" in our hearts and ultimately come out of our mouths and form actions. Words and actions are closely connected by intentions thus providing a basis for judgment.

Love does not take into account a wrong suffered. Love is not keeping score of the sins of others in order to judge and criticize those who have caused harm. One of the classic cases of control is to place oneself as the victim in a relationship with another. Their sin has victimized you and therefore they owe you and once that occurs, they can never seem to pay you back completely. This method of lordship is designed to subtly place you in a superior position forever because the other person inflicted irreparable damage on you. This method of manipulation mistakenly assumes that Our Heavenly Father cannot fully restore you after the damage was done.

I knew of a young couple who fell in love and were married and everything was going well until the husband developed a drug habit. He became consumed with his addiction and the wife suffered. Rather than seek help, they both covered up the situation as though it would go away without any counseling. Rather than crying out to the immediate family for help, the wife thought that she could control the situation and force the husband to quit only to find that he would habitually lie about his addiction. This illusion went on for years until finally she kicked him out of the house. This reality check forced him to seek professional help and he went into rehabilitation. After several months he wanted to reconcile and return home only to find her now playing the "victim" card with him and the rest of the family. By them extending the problem over time, a root of bitterness and ill-will develops. The wife asks herself the question, "If he truly loves me, why does he continue with this addiction?" As time passes her anger deepens and bitterness takes hold. Now they both have a problem. She justifies her bitterness by his addiction and his addiction becomes an escape from the problems in their marriage. Their marriage spirals down into the depths of despair. Only by Love and forgiveness could their marriage be healed.

The writer of Hebrews shares the following:

Hebrews 10:15-17:

15 But the Holy Spirit also witnesses to us; for after He had said before,

16 "This is the covenant that I will make with them after those days, says the LORD: I will put My laws into their hearts, and in their minds I will write them,"

17 then He adds, "Their sins and their lawless deeds I will remember no more." (NKJV)

Our Heavenly Father's Laws reflect His character and as He puts those laws in our hearts and in our minds, we will become like him. One of His characteristics is the full forgiveness of others' sins to the point of removing them from memory. In the Old Testament, there was no eternal orientation to the judgment of sin. When you broke the law, there were specific remedies that were of finite consequences and burning in hell forever was not one of them. How could the New Covenant execute a greater judgment than the Old? When Love went to the cross and accepted all of the sin of the world, the New Covenant was perfected by the blood of the innocent Lamb of God. This sacrifice satisfied the law written in Love for our benefit. On the day of Resurrection, the fulfillment was completed to establish a path of reconciliation for all mankind. Just as Adam walked with God for 33 ½ years then imputed mortality to mankind, Jesus walked 33 ½ years in mortality and then imputed eternal life to mankind.

The earthly ministry of Jesus opened our eyes to our relationship with Our Heavenly Father. Prior to the ministry of Jesus, the Lord God Almighty was thought to be a disciplinarian just waiting for mankind to screw up so that HE could execute judgment. HE was the "enforcer". Man could not comprehend the character of Love at that time due to his sinful nature blinding his eyes and closing his ears to revelation. Out of Love, Our Heavenly Father would send prophets to warn Israel of impending disaster if they continued on their path toward destruction. Since the people did not want to hear correction, they simply killed the prophets thinking that would take care of the problem. How often do we try to kill the messenger when Our Heavenly Father is communicating a warning to us?

People mistakenly believe that by walking in Love you will no longer experience problems. Mankind wants to live in a problem free environment without having to overcome any obstacles or challenges. As long as we are in these human bodies and are subject to the natural laws, there will be things and people to overcome.

Chapter 10

LOVE DOES NOT REJOICE IN UNRIGHTEOUSNESS

*T*here is no joy in suffering and Love does not rejoice when bad things happen to people. There are laws created for our protection and when those laws are broken, suffering ensues. Our Heavenly Father put those laws in place not to lie in waiting for us to break them so He could execute judgment, but to point us toward safety from the consequences of the laws. Every parent who loves their child establishes household laws for the safety and protection of all the members of the family. Restricting children from the cleaning chemicals is for their own safety, not to punish them. When the child breaks that law, the parent must correct the child for his or her lawlessness. It does not bring joy to the parent to cause the child to suffer through the correction but it is necessary for the child to learn and remember that crucial law.

Rejoicing in an injustice indicates the person is vindictive toward the recipients of the injustice. When there is evil or an injustice done, nobody comes out ahead. Someone always loses when unrighteousness is carried out and unfortunately that loss will come back to the instigator as a judgment that requires payment for the injustice done. There are some people who are envious of others that almost get "giddy" when they see harm done to someone they dislike. Deep down inside they want to get even with that person even though they may not be personally acquainted with them. They believe that when another person is brought under some type of judgment, it somehow justifies their inability to walk in the blessings of Our Heavenly Father. Personal regret is not an excuse to gloat when another falls into ruin from some unrighteous act.

There are six hundred thirteen commandments and statutes in the Old Testament. I dare say that any of us could not keep all those commandments for any period of time before we become guilty of breaking them. However, Jesus simplified the Law for us:

Mat 22:35-40:

35 Then one of them, a lawyer, asked Him a question, testing Him, and saying,

36 "Teacher, which is the great commandment in the law?"

37 Jesus said to him, "You shall love the LORD your God with all your heart, with all your soul, and with all your mind.'

38 "This is the first and great commandment.

39 "And the second is like it: 'You shall love your neighbor as yourself.'

40 "On these two commandments hang all the Law and the Prophets." (NKJV)

Much of the Old Testament is made up of the Law and the Prophets and Jesus just summed up all of those books with one word: Love. Unrighteousness is an alternative to Love and thus Love will never rejoice in iniquity. How can I keep the Commandments of Our Heavenly Father? Walk in Love. Those who study the Old Testament in its greatest detail are looking at the foreshadow of the New Testament. The Prophets were prophesying of Jesus and His ultimate sacrifice of Love at the Cross. The Law required a spotless sacrificial lamb to shed blood for the whole world. Jesus could not be lawless in any way. To put it simply, he needed to walk in love 100% of the time, which he did. He wept over the multitudes who surely had sin in their lives. He never rejoiced in iniquity. After all, He came not to condemn the world but that the world through Him might be saved.

Will Love operate in the midst of lawlessness? The answer is "yes", Love supersedes the law and thus will operate even among workers of iniquity. Love was the motivation behind the Ten Commandments to guide and protect the children of Israel. Today, little is understood about the motivation behind Our Heavenly Father creating those detailed statutes found in Leviticus. For example, the food laws included the restriction of eating pork. In America, over the last fifty years pork has become the primary breakfast meat and pizza topping. Do you think that Our Heavenly Father who created the swine would purposefully dangle their meat before us only to demand we abstain from its meat? Pigs do not discern what they intake and are effective garbage disposals. Their digestive tract will allow them to consume harmful bacteria without side effects. However when we consume their meat, not all of those 150+ types of bacteria are killed by heat. Thus when we eat pork, we expose our bodies to bacteria and other toxins that require our immune systems to work overtime. Over time this will have an adverse physiological effect on our body. Our ignorance of this food law is not a license to deem it antiquated.

Is the power of GOD made of none effect when lawless men seek to operate in the gifts of GOD? The Words of GOD contain power even when spoken by lawless men. Those words have intent of Love behind them and even when spoken by workers of iniquity, those words will not return void. Jesus made this quite clear in the following passage:

Matthew 7:21-23:

21 "Not everyone who says to Me, 'Lord, Lord,' will enter the kingdom of heaven, but he who does the will of My Father who is in heaven {will enter.}

22 "Many will say to Me on that day, 'Lord, Lord, did we not prophesy in Your name, and in Your name cast out demons, and in Your name perform many miracles?'

23 "And then I will declare to them, 'I never knew you; DEPART FROM ME, YOU WHO PRACTICE LAWLESSNESS.' (NASB)

In the above passage, there are men who prophesy, cast demons out, and perform miracles, all in the name of Jesus. The power of GOD was in operation among these men but then Jesus makes a bold statement, "Depart from me, you who practice lawlessness"! What a multi-faceted revelation! The power of GOD is not restricted to those who have mastered righteousness. Prophecy, casting out of demons, and miracles are not subject to the lawlessness of the person who performed these gifts from Our Heavenly Father. This would certainly explain why evangelists who have been found to be severely flawed at a personal level could still have positive results in their meetings. THANK GOD that their hidden sins did not keep millions from coming to Christ. The power of Love is greater than any man's sin and will operate even in the midst of lawlessness. After all, we all fall short of the Glory of GOD.

During the age of Pentecost, the church has operated with leaven also known as "sin". In the majesty of the ages, the three feasts of Israel represent three specific time spans. We have been experiencing that age of Pentecost where the church was prophesied to operate with "sin in the camp". What does this mean? The church would grow because Love abounds more than sin can abound. Even though the church flourished, sin would be found at all levels. It mattered not what position or place a person held in the church, sin could be found lurking in the deeper recesses of that person's life. How many times has each of us found the need to repent? Only by the great grace and mercy of Our Loving Heavenly Father have we been restored to fellowship with Him.

It is important that you understand the difference between being lawless and practicing lawlessness. We are all guilty of lawlessness. The difference comes when we are exposed to Love and the law, then we persist in our lawless behavior without restraint or remorse. Habitually walking in lawlessness demands righteous judgment by Our Heavenly Father and that ultimately leads to a cleansing operation. When is the line crossed between being lawless and practicing lawlessness? I don't know but I would ask the question: "Why find out?" Knowing there is the risk of evoking judgment and being required to depart from Our Lord Jesus Christ, pursue Love and you will not have to find out. Can you imagine the sorrow of having the Son of The Most High God tell you to depart from Him? This departure is not forever but only until His righteous judgment corrects and cleanses you of your lawlessness.

Self interest is taking advantage of opportunities without regard for the consequences for others. It ultimately moves toward selfishness and unrighteous. The direction of self interest is away from Love. Disregard of the impact of your actions on others is simply pure selfishness. This immature act is not unexpected of a child who has had no life experiences that impact others. But for the rest of us, there is no excuse for the self absorbed acts that cause others to cry in their pillows at night. Throughout history governments have started out serving the people only to move towards a policy of self interest thereby alienating the people. Once the people had been exploited on a consistent basis, a tipping point occurred and a revolt of the government took place causing the demise of that form of government. If only a government were based on Love, the people's interest would be placed above the interest of those who were selected to hold office. You can better appreciate the Lord's Prayer where "Thy Kingdom come, Thy Will be done".

Lev 19:15:
'You shall do no injustice in judgment. You shall not be partial to the poor, nor honor the person of the mighty. In righteousness you shall judge your neighbor. (NKJV)

The first use of "unrighteousness" in Scripture is the above passage. Unrighteous judgment is a key issue to Our Heavenly Father and Jesus reiterated the importance of this concern. This form of judgment feeds the ego, exploits the weak and poor, and exalts the mighty. It perpetuates a system of unrighteous activity and moves man's reliance inward thus feeding man's ego rather than promoting a relationship with Our Heavenly Father. When man is left to his own devices, death and destruction occur. The ego's self interest cycle will always suck the life out of any situation. On the other hand, when the ego is put in check and made a servant, life springs forth and creates an environment where the weak become strong and the poor are blessed with abundance. Once Love is fully revealed and embraced, scarcity will no longer be an issue on earth. When the righteous man sees a need, he will seek Our Heavenly Father for the honest way to satisfy that need, whether it occurs by multiplying fishes or discovering a new form of energy. The following is a quote from Jesus:

John 7:18:
He that speaketh of himself seeketh his own glory: but

he that seeketh his glory that sent him, the same is true, and no unrighteousness is in him. (KJV)

Jesus spoke only the words He heard from His Father and thus He knew that only Our Heavenly Father's perfect plan, will, and purpose would be done. This is the only way we can be sure that we walk in righteousness and in Love. As we spend time communing with Our Heavenly Father, we become like Him, we Love like Him, and we respond like Him. When we take on His attributes, all of Heaven is at our "beck and call". Jesus had the resources of the Kingdom available to Him at all times. His ministry was to be an example of how Love operates and with what resources it would muster to satisfy the needs of the people. On the other hand, unrighteousness locks up the Kingdom of God and forces mankind to operate under the natural law of decay and destruction. You would think that mankind would get the message! Man's desire to judge by self interest has been a strong force dating back to the expulsion from the Garden. Jesus warned us many times of judging others because He understood the path to unrighteousness was by carnal, self motivated judgment; and unrighteousness ultimately would lead to death and destruction.

Chapter 11

LOVE REJOICES IN TRUTH

*L*ove operates in truth whereas the ego operates in a counterfeit reality. Truth is supported by facts and reality but having all the facts does not necessarily mean you have the truth of the matter. Intent or motive must be considered as well. A key ingredient to the truth is joy. Can you ultimately rejoice or be full of joy when you present the truth? The ultimate goal of truth is unity and if the facts you seek to employ result in division, you are not motivated by Love. Where there is Love and truth, joy abounds.

The legal profession has often used facts and the legal system to subvert the truth. Business professionals know that frequently the outcome of a case is determined by the best attorney, not the truth. Judges also have the ability to sway a jury by which facts they will allow the jury to hear or see. Righteous judgment has its foundation in truth and reality. In the United States, judges are charged with protecting the presumed innocence even though in some venues, compromise may have crept into the minds of judges. Note that the judicial system is based on unity, not division. The expectation of a truthful and righteous outcome is based on the jury deliberating all the facts and deciding a verdict in unity. However, the system has found a way to sanitize the facts to sway the jury by rejection of testimony, witnesses, or the judge's own prejudice. Righteous judgment calls for truth and rejoices in it without prejudice.

Facts can harm people when presented without Love. How often have we been open with the facts, knowing that they would hurt the recipient? This act of division is the ego's attempt to establish lordship over the recipient. The motive for this type of behavior is self interest. This person's position may be one of desperation, frustration, or simply the desire for control. In my younger years, I mastered the ability to assimilate facts that served my position and was able to present a superior argument even though I was wrong. I was winning the battle but losing the war. I was trained to be competitive at a young age and one by-product was the need to always win an argument whether I was right or wrong, also known as the "my way or the highway" doctrine. I would unknowingly damage my relationship with others when I walked this path. Oh how our egos will deceive us!

Illusion differs from counterfeit reality in that illusions are meant to be temporary perceptions without attempting to convince the observer of a new reality. For instance, businesspeople promote themselves by "dressing for success". Their individual characteristics are reflected by their choices in clothing and accessories. As long as they do not attempt to become someone else, there is no counterfeiting. Our wardrobes are designed to project different illusions based on the occasion and audience. On the other hand, counterfeit reality attempts to replace truth and reality and requires substantial energy and resources to keep the counterfeit alive. Complexities are built around the counterfeit to sustain and defend it to the bitter end.

John 8:31-32:
31 Jesus therefore said to those Jews that had believed him, If ye abide in my word, (then) are ye truly my disciples;
32 and ye shall know the truth, and the truth shall make you free. (ASV)

Jesus shared a very important truth here- the truth will set you free of bondage. The bondage may be an illusion, a doctrine, a perception, or ignorance. His Word was from Our Heavenly Father who speaks pure truth without any variance. As we pursue a close relationship with Our Heavenly Father, truth will begin to flourish in our lives. Like peeling away an onion, our own false beliefs will be revealed to us so that they may be discarded, one by one. The outer shell of our counterfeit reality is targeted first, the most obvious false doctrines. We may attempt to cling to those doctrines at first for they have provided us comfort over the years and may have been instituted by our earthly parents. As a child clings to the comfort of his or her baby blanket, there is a point where the childish things must be put away. False doctrines serve only to keep you from the intimate relationship you truly desire. As you release those beliefs the Holy Spirit draws you closer to the Holy of Holies located in your Temple. No sin is allowed in the Holy of Holies and you must give up all falsehoods at the door.

Many of us have been taught that you must have an intercessor between you and Our Heavenly Father but that is not true. Moses interceded for the children of Israel only because they did not seek a direct relationship with Our Heavenly Father.

Exodus 20:18-19:

18 Now all the people witnessed the thunderings, the lightning flashes, the sound of the trumpet, and the mountain smoking; and when the people saw it, they trembled and stood afar off.

19 Then they said to Moses, "You speak with us, and we will hear; but let not God speak with us, lest we die." (NKJV)

The people could not see the truth of the Love of Our Heavenly Father but were blinded by their fear and insecurity to the point they wanted Moses to be their intercessor. Love delivered them out of Egypt and brought them to the holy mountain but they grew up in an environment of fear, unbelief, and oppression. The Egyptians had ingrained fear and unworthiness in the people thus causing them to look at their Deliverer in a similar manner. Even though they had been freed, they still lived in the bondage of their minds. The generation who fled Egypt was unable to enter the Promised Land. Their ingrained fear and unbelief kept them from truly being free.

Our mind is not our ally but should be our servant. When we spend our life building up our mind and letting our spirit man grow dormant, our mind will take control and become a taskmaster similar to the Egyptians. Our ego will become dominant and use truth only to perpetuate its agenda. Our ego operates whether we are in control of thousands or in the slum. Its goal is only to perpetuate an illusion, not reality. This counterfeit reality becomes our "blanket" of comfort even though we may be wallowing in the mud. As we begin to dwell on a closer relationship with Our Heavenly Father, truth begins to show up on the scene. Just as a seed germinates, the truth begins to bring forth shoots of life to your situation. Truth challenges the counterfeit reality which has been like a wall keeping you in the status quo. Then suddenly you realize that you do not have to live this way anymore and Love draws you out of the lifeless trap that has held you by your own illusions.

Luke 15:14-20:

14 "But when he had spent all, there arose a severe famine in that land, and he began to be in want.

15 "Then he went and joined himself to a citizen of that country, and he sent him into his fields to feed swine.

16 "And he would gladly have filled his stomach with the pods that the swine ate, and no one gave him anything.

17 "But when he came to himself, he said, 'How many of my father's hired servants have bread enough and to spare, and I perish with hunger!

18 'I will arise and go to my father, and will say to him, "Father, I have sinned against heaven and before you,

19 "and I am no longer worthy to be called your son. Make me like one of your hired servants."'

20 "And he arose and came to his father. But when he was still a great way off, his father saw him and had compassion, and ran and fell on his neck and kissed him. (NKJV)

In the above parable, Jesus provides us another multifaceted view of life. The son had recklessly spent his inheritance and was now living among the swine which he believed was his new reality. When he came to his senses he realized that even his father's servants were better off than him. What happened? His eyes were opened with a revelation about his situation and the true reality flooded his awareness. Did the father change at that moment? No, the son came to the realization that his situation was subject to change. Upon his return, his father had mercy on him, was filled with joy, and threw a party for him. The son rediscovered the truth in his relationship with his father and their relationship was restored.

In Deuteronomy 29:4, we are told: "Yet the LORD hath not given you an heart to perceive, and eyes to see, and ears to hear, unto this day " Why would Our Heavenly Father hold back revelation? The young son was not interested in his father's wisdom but wanted his portion of inheritance to go off and have a good time. After he squandered his wealth, a severe famine spread across the land and he suffered its effects. Was it a famine of "hearing God's voice?" How many of us have distanced ourselves from Our Heavenly Father only to find that in the outer darkness we suffer the effects of a famine, whether it be physical, financial, emotional, or spiritual? As we decided that we knew what was best for us, we headed out on a journey away from Our Heavenly Father only to find that in His Presence was fulfillment. Once we repent (turn back toward Our Heavenly Father) do our eyes and ears open thus realizing the error of our ways.

In the parable, the father honored the son's will in allowing him to take his inheritance and squander it. The father knew that the son's immaturity would prevail and thus lose his inheritance but he honored the son's request. How many young people believe that they are indestructible and know more than their fathers only to find themselves soon living among the swine! The love of the father moved him with mercy once he saw that the son's eyes had been opened and that the son was ready to have "ears to hear".

Rejoicing in the truth brings forth maturity. Are you being tossed to and fro by every wind of doctrine? Are you running here and there looking for revelation? Revelation is to be found in your closet, not a thousand miles away in another meeting! Church is for fellowship with others, the closet is for separating yourself and conversing with Our Heavenly Father. 100% pure truth is spoken by Our Heavenly Father and as you listen to Him, His truths will permeate your soul and your spirit will rejoice by being set free of those counterfeit realities that your ego has been clinging to throughout most of your life. As the truth permeates every aspect of your life, your outlook will change and you will move toward optimism that Our Heavenly Father REALLY has everything under control. People will detect this truth emanating from the center of your being and will be at ease when they are around you. You will then understand how the truth can set you free!

Chapter 12

LOVE BEARS ALL THINGS

"To bear" means to deck, thatch, to cover a roof. It also means to protect or keep and preserve by covering, to cover over with silence, to keep secret, to hide, or to conceal the errors and faults of others. By covering Love keeps something away which threatens, to bear up against, hold out against, and so endure, to forbear. How would you like to have someone on your side to "bear" all things on your behalf. You do! His name is Jesus and he bore ALL your sins at the cross to enable you be reconciled unto Our Heavenly Father. For those of you who have children, you have been exposed to this aspect of love. As you nurtured your child, you were the child's protector against all threats. As your child grew, his or her mobility increased but the child always knew where their safe place was at, next to their parent. You acted as their "shelter".

The centerpiece of love is forgiveness. In order to bear all things love must be able to forgive the errors, weakness, and ignorance of the person being "covered". As we mature in Christ, we begin to understand mankind and the part ego plays in each person. As we observe actions of others, we can understand the underlying motivating factors that direct their behavior. Our continuous forgiving attitude will defend the relationship with the other person thus allowing us to minister life and loving correction to them.

Love has endurance. This becomes abundantly clear when you raise children. When they are young you overlook their immaturity but as they become teenagers, you begin to expect "irresponsibility" to change to "responsibility". This stage of their development uncovers your stage of development being able to "bear all things". This love provides a steady, consistent defense to the loved one in spite of the actions of the other person.

When you bear another's burden, you take the weight of that burden because the other person is unable to carry it. The burden is passed from the weak to the strong, from the uninformed to the wise. Jesus bore our burdens before we accepted Him. We did not deserve to have our burdens removed from us but His Love understood what needed to be done on our behalf to insure our reconciliation to Our Heavenly Father. Love motivated Him to take on our burden and reverse the curse of the law.

Most Christians have a problem in understanding that the pursuit of Love requires one to expect conflict, difficulty, and pressure. There is this one-sided view that Love only involves a non-confrontational happiness like an angel playing a harp on a fluffy cloud without a care in the world. Love is so much more. When Love bears a burden it creates pressure which in turn creates growth on the person who is bearing the burden. Love overcomes the challenge with right thinking and response. It sees no need to exploit others when these challenges come but sees a way to help promote growth in the recipients. Conflict necessitates a mediation based on Love's expected outcome. While man's conflict promotes death and destruction, Love seeks to reconcile and restore to unity. Restoration may be an extended process of months or years but nonetheless, Love seeks unity.

Love's ability to bear and cover is a sign of strength and tenacity. Those attributes are often assigned to warriors or competitors but their attributes tend to fail with age whereas the same attributes of Love tend to increase with age and maturity. The walk of Love includes acts of service where the one you serve is much weaker than you. Your strength makes up for the other's weakness. When I was a little boy my mother signed my brother up for drum lessons once a week. She did not drive nor did we have a second car so the three of us made our weekly trek to the instructor's house. We had to carry the snare drum back and forth. First, my brother would carry the drum on this lengthy walk. Soon he would tire out and my mother would happily tote the drum while walking with her two boys. Occasionally I would try to get in on the action but that was short lived. Out of her love for my brother was my mother willing to make the walk lugging around that snare drum. It was not unusual for us to walk at least one half mile to our destination whether it be the shopping center or a drum lesson.

The third feast given to Israel was the Feast of Booths or Tabernacles. This feast was known for its "booths" or temporary covering where the person entered into the "covering". I believe this "covering" is one of Love where the booth represents the bearing or "thatching" of the covering. A thatched roof such as the ones you see in England are used even today and provide complete protection from the elements. Love will be the basis of protection as the third feast is played out on the world stage.

Love bears the responsibility of walking in true reality. Some people live in a counterfeit reality produced by their misguided beliefs that they are somebody other than their true self. Taking on the characteristics of a cowboy as an illusion is nothing more than an expression of emotion. You may wear the hat and the boots but that doesn't make you a cowboy although it does show one of the many facets of your personality. If you dressed up like a cowboy and attempted to ride a bull, your counterfeit reality would not keep you from being thrown by the bull. The bull knows his job! Many people try to sustain a counterfeit reality by walking out someone else's life. Love will intervene and will bear the task of setting things strait with truth and compassion. Love does not have to keep up with the Joneses but promotes gratitude for a person's station in life.

The ego does not want to bear all things but wants others to bear the responsibilities and accountability. The ego wants to be king and have a house full of servants to see to every need. The ultimate consequence of this path is boredom. What happens when you have the biggest house, the most toys, the most servants, and the most vacations? Life becomes meaningless. Why? Life is all about relationships, not things. The quest of the ego is always out of reach whether it be a bigger house, a faster car, or a more exotic vacation. Men want to display their trophies for all to see and envy. Once you have all the things, what else is there to acquire? Fulfillment in life does not come by how many "big boy toys" you have accumulated.

Being able to bear all things denotes an underlying strength that supersedes the strength found in other walks of life. What people have not fully understood is that when you walk in Love, there is an immeasurable resource available to you. How could Jesus bare the sins of the world on the cross? We know so little about this event other than a somewhat short description of His act. This had to be the greatest act of any person at any time on earth yet we know so little of how He was able to endure and complete this calling. His strength came from the Love that allowed Him to bear the brunt of all sin for all time committed by all of mankind. There was not one sin of any generation left out. Love made sure of that. Why? It is not Our Heavenly Father's plan that any should perish but have everlasting life no matter how long it takes for the truth to be revealed. Surely Love would be more successful than allowing 95% of the world's population to burn forever in a hell based on torture!

"You owe me." Those are the infamous words of the ego as it pursues a position of power over others. The Lord's Prayer in Matthew Chapter 6 includes "And forgive us our debts, as we forgive our debtors". Love bears the debts of the debtors thus allowing the debtor to learn from the debt without paying the full judgment of the debt. Love promotes a jubilee in our lives thus allowing us to repent of the direction which created the debt and turn to a life free of the debt. Have you ever noticed that when you loan someone money your relationship with them changes? The debtor is servant to the lender and when your relationship contains this aspect, your brother becomes your servant and will tend to distance himself from you when he has difficulty in paying you back. Nobody wants to be confronted with failure, especially financial failure. How do you restore your brother? Love forgives the debt. When you forgive the debt, you open up the windows of Heaven to pour out a blessing on your storehouse. Love honors those who are full of grace and are merciful toward those who have yet to mature in wisdom and understanding. The following Scripture provides clarity as to how loves responds and is rewarded:

1Peter 3:8-9:
8 Finally, all of you be of one mind, having compassion for one another; love as brothers, be tenderhearted, be courteous;
9 not returning evil for evil or reviling for reviling, but on the contrary blessing, knowing that you were called to this, that you may inherit a blessing.

An alternative to bearing all things is to judge and distance yourself from the issues at hand. Out of sight and out of mind do not work! When you attempt to interrupt the flow of life by creating a vacuum by distance and judgment, the vacuum gets filled with the very thing you attempted to remove. In Luke Chapter 11, Jesus spoke a parable concerning the casting out of unclean spirits by two separate motivations: one by the finger of God, the other by Beelzebub. If the unclean spirit is cast out by the kingdom of Satan, the house is divided with a result of the return of the unclean spirit with seven other spirits. However if the unclean spirit is cast out by love and replaced with the Kingdom of God then there is no vacuum created for the unclean spirit to return. Man's judgment and division creates a vacuum and it will be filled. This reality is behind the generational curses that repeat themselves over and over until someone comes forth and breaks those curses by Love. You cannot deny the context of your history. Our Heavenly Father put you on this earth through your mother and father and all of their history for a reason. Rather than reject your history and theirs, you should learn from this context which is a sign of wisdom. You must allow forgiveness to play its role in taking away the pain created by the history you inherited. When Love bears all things, there is no vacuum to fill.

Ephesians 5:20 giving thanks always for all things to God the Father in the name of our Lord Jesus Christ,

When we are called to bear all things we must remember that Our Heavenly Father has accountability for the entire earth. Nothing happens without His Knowledge. He will not allow us to be placed in any situation beyond our resources even though there are times when we may feel that we are all alone. With this understanding we can truly give thanks always for all things knowing that Our Heavenly Father has things in control and that ultimately Love will prevail in our particular situation.

Love is the bond of perfection as Paul tells us in Colossians Chapter 3. Isn't a mature and perfected walk the very thing we seek? In order to receive this walk we must put on tender mercies, kindness, humility, meekness, longsuffering, bearing with one another, and forgiving one another. But above all these things put on love, which is the bond of perfection.

Jesus tells us to Love our enemies, bless them that curse you, do good to them that hate you, and pray for them which despitefully use you and persecute you. This will lead to being perfect, even as Our Heavenly Father is perfect. We are only perfect through Love, not by any other means; not by works, not by repetitive confession, only by pursuing Love. When we truly love our enemies, they can be converted to our friends. An enemy is at odds with you for some reason. The source of the conflict may be an uninformed decision, scarcity, misunderstanding, or insensitivity to another's need. If an ego is involved, Our Heavenly Father may find it necessary to execute judgment to correct the illusion that the person is living under. For whatever reason, Love will find a way to convert the enemy and restore the relationship and time is not an issue with Love for it is not confined to time.

The essence of Love bearing all things can be found in the sacred bond of marriage. The Sixth Commandment "You shall not commit adultery" explicitly covers this bond. It represents the bond of Our Heavenly Father and mankind. The Old Testament was based on "if" where if the children of Israel kept the Covenant, then they would be blessed. When Love went to the Cross, a New Covenant was consummated and "if" was removed from the relationship, the essence of unconditional Love. Since mankind could not keep the Old Covenant, Jesus removed the dependency by bringing forth an unconditional covenant which eliminated the weakest link- mankind. His bearing of all sin did not require you or me to perform, He completed the work and imparted the fullness of unconditional Love making it available to every person on earth.

As our eyes are opened to the faithfulness of Our Heavenly Father toward us, we will begin to comprehend how Love bears all things. In the Old Testament, Israel was unfaithful to Our Heavenly Father and committed "adultery" by seeking after other gods and idols. He was forced to divorce Israel in keeping with His Law. However that marriage was replaced by another marriage and a better covenant. This new marriage did not require the bride to perform in order to consummate the marriage. Only the bridegroom had to commit. This eliminated the possibility for divorce since the bridegroom became fully accountable for the bond of marriage to stay intact. The unconditional Love of Jesus would bear all things and cover all sins so that the bride could live eternally with the bridegroom. This sacred bond cannot be broken and the kindness and tenderness is expressed each time we sin and seek forgiveness. Once you can fully grasp this reality, you will begin to change and start living a life of gratitude. Each time you sin, you will immediately seek grace and mercy from Our Heavenly Father so that there will be nothing to restrict your fellowship. As we begin to understand the sacred marriage with the Creator of the universe, our eyes will be opened to the power of Love and will begin to operate in that power to bear the burdens of the weak. Think about it.

Chapter 13

LOVE BELIEVES ALL THINGS

*T*o believe is to think to be true, to be persuaded of, to credit, place confidence in, or to entrust. A typical four year old child believes all things. The child's formative years have been protected by the nurturing parents and all external influences are believed to be true. The child has had little or no exposure to lies, misrepresentations, or misleading acts. This child has been protected by Love and is open to consume all outside stimuli filtered by the parents. What a fertile ground of learning! Once again we understand why we should be as children to enter in to the Kingdom of Heaven. The child has consistently trusted the parents' words and actions in a safe environment. How much more nurturing is Our Heavenly Father toward each of us!

Believing and trusting go hand in hand and both are clothed in truth. When Jesus was approached by the centurion about healing his servant in Matthew Chapter 8, He simply spoke the word of healing over the servant. The centurion believed that the word was sufficient and the servant would be healed. Jesus did not have to go and physically touch the servant. The centurion was a man of authority and understood authority. He believed Jesus to be "Lord" and that belief was sufficient. He trusted the word of Jesus and either saw or heard of all the healings that were occurring. Beliefs, trust, and truth are all followed by acts of confirmation and you can be sure that our beliefs will be tested. The Spirit of God is not restricted by space or time and thus the healing of the servant was immediate.

I believe that we were created to believe all things. Faith and courage are required to start a new business venture, buy a house on credit, or bring a new child into the world. How are we going to be able to provide for the child? Will we make the right decisions for the child? The list goes on. Love takes up the gap in those times of uncertainty. We must believe that Our Heavenly Father will intervene on our behalf and see us through any hard times that come. As we look around us and see that others have overcome similar obstacles, our belief system becomes stronger and gives us confidence that we too will overcome. Our family and friends encourage and strengthen our belief system. Life's experiences strengthen our beliefs. Most of all, listening and responding to that still small voice moves us to believing all things. Hearing Our Heavenly Father's voice generates faith, and faith generates actions with results, and that is how mankind progresses.

As we acquire wisdom and understanding we can appreciate the need to believe all things. As we mature, we are better able to implement our beliefs that are enshrouded with goodness. That is what makes a man or woman great.

We truly believe that "I can do all things through Christ who strengthens me" (Philippians 4:13). In that passage, Paul shared that he was content no matter what the circumstance whether he had plenty or had nothing. Of course it is easier to believe when you have plenty but the test of your beliefs come when you have nothing. When you believe all things you know that your circumstances are subject to change even if it takes a miracle. When you mix your calling with your ability to believe all things, you have tapped into the empowerment given to you by Our Heavenly Father to manifest that calling. Each person arrives at that realization at a different point in their walk.

"I'll believe when I see it" and "seeing is believing" are two phrases that limit Love in your life. A miracle is a marvelous event manifesting a supernatural act of Our Heavenly Father and it supersedes the natural course of events. For instance, at the age of nineteen my wife's leg was measured by a podiatrist to be shorter than the other leg and he was going to order an insert for her shoes to compensate for the difference. She went to a Bible study with a friend and there was a time of prayer afterwards. The minister who was conducting the meeting asked for prayer requests and she asked if he would pray for her leg to be lengthened. She had said to herself, "Father, if you can heal me, I want to see it". So the minister had her sit in a chair with all gathered around and lifted her two feet together for all to see the discrepancy. Yes, they were of different lengths. So he prayed. Just as Our Heavenly Father lengthened her leg for all to see, He closed her eyes. It was indeed a miracle and confirmed by the podiatrist. Her eyes were closed to make a point that Our Heavenly Father does not perform miracles to prove that He can. His Love for her was enough to lengthen her leg and reveal to her and all who watched of His Love and power.

Jesus did not heal everyone during His earthly ministry. He only healed those whom Our Heavenly Father instructed Him to heal. As children we wanted someone else to do all the work for us for we did not understand the need to grow and mature. As we have been put into times of testing, we come out on the other side stronger and hopefully wiser. As we grow in wisdom, understanding, knowledge, and skill we can begin to grasp how Our Heavenly Father expects us to "believe all things". I am convinced that until we believe all things through the eyes of Love, the current social and economic system will prevail.

Faith and hope play an important role of believing all things. Hope establishes a direction or focus and faith provides the action or momentum toward the manifestation.

Hebrews 11:1:
Now faith is the substance of things hoped for, the evidence of things not seen. (KJV)

Where the church has missed the mark in the faith walk, Love must enter into the picture as a precursor to hope. When hope and faith are focused on producing a counterfeit reality, Our Heavenly Father will not honor the prayer or manifestation of the hope. The so called "name it and claim it" attitude left Love out of the equation. Our Heavenly Father will honor requests where Love is the focus and the outcome is based on the reality that Love must operate in to fulfill the calling of the person. That is why it is critical to spend time in your closet to seek out the will of Our Heavenly Father in your life. When you do this hope is initiated. Next, there needs to be power and authority applied to this hope given:

Romans 10:17:
So then faith [cometh] by hearing, and hearing by the word of God. (KJV)

When Our Heavenly Father speaks, power and authority are manifested in Heaven AND the earth. HIS words have the power to create and Love is transformed from spirit to matter.

Scientists have discovered the "God particle", the smallest particle of matter. This particle has always been around, we simply did not have the instrumentation or perspective to observe or perceive it. This particle is thought to transition between matter and a wave form. I suspect that it really transitions between matter and spirit form. This in part would explain how Love can manifest in spirit then on earth. When the miracle of conception occurs, our spiritual nature with our gifts and callings are imparted from the spirit realm into the physical realm in a moment. Love initiates a new life and purpose into the manifested realm to move mankind forward in some fashion. Like a piece in a jigsaw puzzle, that person plays a critical role. Without that person, the picture will not be complete.

In order to believe all things in Love, you must understand that when trials come Our Heavenly Father has provided a way to overcome those trials. Trials provide opportunities to grow and mature even though most of us would prefer to grow without any pain or stress. Our Heavenly Father encourages us to endure the trial for a season knowing that no trial is beyond our capacity:

1 Corinthians 10:13:
No trial has overtaken you that is not faced by others. And God is faithful: Hewill not let you be tried beyond what you are able to bear, but with the trial will also provide a way out so that you may be able to endure it. (NET)

Our biggest challenge during a trial is our mind. Our mind does not believe all things but believes in a narrowly defined view with two outcomes: success or failure. Love believes in infinite alternatives to the trial or situation. For instance, I had a friend who invested in an oil & gas drilling program with a large exploration company. He got in over his head and owed them $250,000. He only had two choices: come up with the money or file bankruptcy. However, when the day of reckoning came, he walked into their office without the money and before he could tell them of his plan to file bankruptcy, they interrupted him and told him that they decided to forgive the debt without any recourse- a third alternative he had not even considered nor dared to pursue.

When our mind tells us that things look bleak, we must remember that Love bears all things and that Our Heavenly

Father has not abandoned us but is there to guide us through the most challenging of times. For Love to bear all things there must be the tests and trials to bear! When Jesus went to the cross, the ultimate test occurred. When we deal with our daily struggles in life even though they may seem larger than life itself, we can find comfort in Scripture of those who had to bear much greater burdens than us. Our Heavenly Father equipped them to endure those severe trials just as He has equipped us. However, we must be guided by our heart and not our mind. From our heart comes forth the divine intelligence to comprehend all things and all possible solutions to our problems. The mind is only as good as the exposure to information over our lifetime. Our mind has difficulty in understanding infinity and anything it doesn't understand, it really does not embrace when times are tough.

The classic Biblical example of unbelief is the story of Israel's unwillingness of entering into the Promised Land, the land of milk and honey. The original journey should have taken eighteen months. For those who claim seeing is believing, Israel proves that theory wrong. The saw the Red Sea part, pillars of fire and smoke, the glory of the Lord on Moses' face, daily manna, and the Voice of God at Mount Sinai, yet their unbelief prevented them from entering into the Promised Land. They did not comprehend the Love of Our Heavenly Father. Their revelation of Love had been subdued by the harsh acts of Pharaoh and they were unable to receive the blessing of the Promised Land. Their carnal logic was stronger than the voice in their hearts. Except for Joshua and Caleb, none of that generation entered in. It took 38 ½ years for the people to finally receive the blessing and only after the generation of unbelief died off did the children finally enjoy the fruits of the Promised Land.

This unbelief is a lack of faith and causes us to depart from Love. Our Heavenly Father is an all knowing God and there is no unbelief in Heaven. The world of the unseen is greater than the world of the seen. For instance, you cannot see ultraviolet waves but they are measurable and affect our daily lives. Unbelief questions Love and its ability to perform for the benefit of mankind. Behind every miracle of Jesus was the Love of Our Heavenly Father and unbelief had a negative impact on the mighty works that Jesus did:

Matthew 13:58:
And he did not many mighty works there because of their unbelief.

In Matthew Chapter 17, Jesus was confronted by His disciples concerning their inability to cast out a devil in a young boy. He pointed to their unbelief and the fact that faith was necessary to cast out the devil. Love and faith work together to change people's lives and to manifest blessings on behalf of Our Heavenly Father. Once Jesus went to the cross and rose from the dead, the disciples experienced a new ministry. Their inability to minister healing was replaced with a power and authority that changed the world. What happened? Jesus tore the veil that separated Our Heavenly Father from us and spent forty days after His resurrection teaching the disciples of this reality. From that point on, the disciples operated in a new anointing and assurance of their ministry and that reality is with us today if we will pursue it.

When Our Heavenly Father speaks to us and tells us that He is going to do something we can be assured that His Love is the motivating force behind His actions. Often His plan will operate in areas we do not understand. Our lack of understanding should not invoke unbelief but when we hear His Word, faith should come forth. What appears to be negative is simply a path to success. The children of Israel had to experience the Wilderness before they could enter into the Promised Land. So often we want the easy path requiring no faith. Without the challenges in life, we cannot appreciate His Love in bringing us through our own wilderness adventure. Everyone wants to feel a sense of accomplishment and that requires us to be stretched and tested that we may grow and mature.

Another aspect of believing all things is understanding authority. When you are given a calling you will be sent to "school" by Our Heavenly Father. You will learn how to apply your gifts, respect the Law, and appreciate the need for grace and mercy. This may take a short period of time to graduate or it could take decades, depending on the calling. As we mature we begin to understand authority and how to operate within the authority given to us. Love does not usurp authority but operates within legitimate authority granted by Our Heavenly Father. This authority may include dealing with devils, healing the sick, or speaking forth funding for the Kingdom. The key to this authority is to hear from Our Heavenly Father. He will tell us to go and do something and His words contain both power and authority. He will open the doors, provide the means, and bring forth Heavenly assistance to bring His Word to pass. Our job is to respond and walk in Love and faith acting upon His Word. Initially, we may be directed to do small tasks on His behalf. It may be to help a stranger or speak a kind word to a hurting friend. As we respond and "walk by the Spirit", our authority is increased for our stewardship has been tested and found to be good. As we expand our expectations to ALL THINGS, we move into fellowship and communion with Our Heavenly Father where there is no unbelief.

It may take courage to walk the path that He puts us on. It may be a seemingly lonely path at times but He is Loving and faithful to meet our every need. As we embrace the Love that believes all things we remove self-imposed limitations that prevent us from fulfilling our calling.

Chapter 14

LOVE HOPES ALL THINGS

*H*ope is an expectation or belief in a positive outcome related to events and circumstances in one's life. We all naturally hope for the best in our lives yet without hope, focus and direction of faith is lost for faith is the substance of things hoped for.

Love is the origin of hope. The phrase "In the beginning, GOD" when added to "GOD is Love" provides us a perspective of when Love became active. GOD'S Love initiated action to create the heavens and the earth and pure hope was the expectation or direction of the outcome with faith being the substance of that hope until manifestation occurred. Hope initiated by Our Heavenly Father is a wondrous thing for its purity allows faith to be produced, the precursor to manifestation. This is why it is so important to have communion with Our Heavenly Father and it is why Jesus' custom was to pray while in His earthly ministry. Putting your hopes into an illusion will produce nothing except disappointment and that is why it is critical to not pursue a counterfeit reality. You might say "How do I know if I am pursuing an illusion?" Did the pursuit come from above? Is it producing good fruit? Is it consuming all my resources without any result? Does this pursuit line up with my passion, gifts, and calling? Misplaced hope can cause you to question your purpose in life so you must ask these questions to assess your direction in life.

Proverbs 13:12:
Hope deferred maketh the heart sick: but [when] the desire cometh, [it is] a tree of life.

Deferred or delay hope weakens a person but as your calling or purpose comes to fruition, it produces a productive life. Our Heavenly Father put hope in each one of us when HE places us on this earth with our calling. That calling is the attraction to those things which enable us to fulfill our calling. When we turn away from the attraction, we weaken and move away from our relationship with Our Heavenly Father. As we pursue our calling we regain our direction or hope and we experience a sense of fulfillment.

Our minds can work against us in pursuing our hopes and dreams. Since our mind is binary in nature, it cannot comprehend multiple scenarios easily. What is binary? "Binary" means there are two choices: yes or no, black or white, up or down, etc. Just as the color spectrum is made of many colors and hues, the scenarios to bring us to our calling are also infinite. Don't worry, Our Heavenly Father has everything under control. As we pursue our hope in the purity and innocence of a small child, we will be guided through the maze of life to pick up the tools and resources we need to fulfill that calling that we arrived in the womb with.

Hope and trust go hand in hand. Can we trust Our Heavenly Father to direct our path of hope to the fulfillment of our calling? Of course! If HE can keep the solar system in place with the highest degree of accuracy, surely HE can be trusted to guide each and every soul on this planet. In the beginning, the Spirit of GOD hovered over the earth and moved chaos into structure. The result was that all came into agreement with Our Heavenly Father's plan and purpose. Set within the Milky Way galaxy among innumerable other galaxies and solar systems, HE focused HIS plan on this planet. Not being a random act, HE put order on this planet and began the process to bring each of us forth into a separate being taken from HIS character for a unique purpose and to experience the Love of communion, fellowship, and service. You only have to look up at night in a secluded place to get a glimpse of the majesty of HIS plan.

Jeremiah 17:7-8:

7 "Blessed is the man who trusts in the LORD, And whose hope is the LORD.

8 For he shall be like a tree planted by the waters, Which spreads out its roots by the river, And will not fear when heat comes; But its leaf will be green, And will not be anxious in the year of drought, Nor will cease from yielding fruit

The prophet Jeremiah spoke by the Spirit of the Lord God Almighty and specifically told us that our hope should be placed in HIM. As we commune with Our Heavenly Father, we will not fear nor will we be anxious when tests and trials present themselves to us and you can be assured they will.

Hope's time frame is the future and is always connected to time itself. Our Heavenly Father operates outside of time and is not restricted to time. That is a reality difficult for us to understand since our view is engulfed in time. Our best understanding comes from the perspective of "time travelers" who are able to hop in a machine or by other means travel through time whether forward or backward. Beyond our understanding is the ramification of changing some act or event that could affect the future. This is not a problem for Our Heavenly Father who knows the beginning from the end and provides us our calling with an adequate amount of hope and direction to pursue it. We can rest in the fact that as we operate within HIS timeframe, there will be no negative consequence to our action. Effectively, we have the advantage of time traveling without having to do it since HE knows the beginning from the end and directs us accordingly. What a deal!

In the above passage, we are told to "fear not" when the heat comes, and I assure you the heat WILL come. We are told to endure when trials and tribulations come our way. These tests are to reveal to us our strengths and weaknesses thus giving us focus during the maturing process. Our awareness of the purpose of the tests that come our way helps us deal with those circumstances in a righteous manner rather than creating a belief that the world is against you and why were you even born! In the Book of Job, Job's example provides us the insight that suffering is part of the big picture and to trust Our Heavenly Father who will work it all out on our behalf.

As we develop endurance, our strength and stamina will grow. Overwhelming trials will become commonplace irritations and non-events. Those worries that kept you awake at night will no longer impact your sleep or your peace. As you mature, others will look to you for direction and comfort for they know of your connection with Our Heavenly Father. Suddenly, a leader of some degree is born. Your leadership may simply be directed toward your family, friends, or business associates, but your hope and direction will be acknowledged.

James 1:12:

Blessed is the man who endures temptation; for when he has been approved, he will receive the crown of life which the Lord has promised to those who love Him (NKJV)

This passage provides us assurance of the blessings of love, hope, and faith. Our revelation of Love and its walk will direct our path of hope. Our faith will allow us to endure through the times of temptation. Upon successful completion of this time of testing, we will receive approval by Our Heavenly Father for the greatest blessing of all: the crown of life. This is the "zoe" life which is a divinely appointed life operating in a manner similar to Jesus in His resurrected body. The ultimate reward of this path is walking in the fullness of Love.

In the Heart of Our Heavenly Father is the source for all

hope. Symbolically the manna found in the Ark of the Covenant represented among other things, hope. Each day Our Heavenly Father provided manna to the children of Israel in the wilderness. The manna was only good for a day, or two if before a Sabbath. There was no hoarding of the manna. Initially, each person in the wilderness exercised hope and faith that our Heavenly Father would provide the next day. After so many days of success, it became familiar and commonplace for the manna to be on the ground. At that point, Our Heavenly Father became the provider of sustenance for the people which in essence provided them with "life". Can you imagine a perfect food to keep you healthy? The people had been enslaved for generations by the Egyptians and needed the revelation of hope in their lives to become real to them. What better way than to start with a basic need- food. The next need was water. When the water was low, Our Heavenly Father had Moses strike the rock and water came gushing out for the people to drink. These acts were designed to provide hope for entrance into the Promised Land. However, of that generation who left Egypt, only two men could overcome the ego's power over them. Joshua and Caleb converted that hope to faith and were able to enter the Promised Land after forty years.

Placing your hope in others can lead to sorrow and disappointment. When your hope is not based or originated in Our Heavenly Father, it is subject to the sin and judgments against the other person. Unfortunately more often than not, you will be disappointed in the result. The complexities of life work against you placing hope in another person.

Sometimes there are just circumstances beyond their control to perform and in the end they will typically do what is necessary for them to survive even if it is an illusion in their mind. Fear can have a significant impact on people and that is why we are urged to "fear not" throughout Scripture. When fear has embraced you, others cannot count on you to perform and fulfill the hope placed in you. Misplaced hope can damage the maturing process of faith and cause you to become cynical towards all people. When that happens, judgment and division creep in and further separates you from Our Heavenly Father. We must keep in mind that HE created all mankind and we must find the lesson to be learned when we encounter disappointment in the hope we placed in others.

The first use of hope in Scripture is seen in the Book of Ruth. There was a famine in the land of Israel, so Ruth's future husband's family went to the land of Moab. Ruth married into the family. During a ten year period, the three men of the family died and left Ruth, her mother-in-law, and sister-in-law in desperation. They were broke, husbandless, and hungry so things were looking a little bleak. Even though Naomi, her mother-in-law, had urged her to go her separate way, Ruth committed to stay with Naomi and receive GOD as her god. They ended up returning to Bethlehem at the beginning of the barley harvest which incidentally refers to the "overcomers" in Scripture. This begins the beautiful love story based on hope and redemption. Ruth goes to a local field being harvested hoping to pick up any grain left by the harvesters. Boaz, the owner the field, sees

Ruth and is attracted to her immediately. It turns out that Boaz is able to redeem Ruth and marry her. Ruth conceives a child who turns out to be the grandfather of King David.

This story reflects the bigger picture of Our Heavenly Father's plan. Little did Ruth know that she would become the wife of Boaz. Back in Moab, her life looked like it was pretty well over. Once Ruth accepted Our Heavenly Father as her God, her hope was activated and the future began to unfold. Ruth was called to be King David's great grandmother. Little did she know when she was enduring the famine back in Moab that her destiny would be so bright!

Are you in a famine of some type? Know that your present circumstances do not define your future. The next phone call or face to face encounter could change the course of your life. As our journey through this life progresses, our path appears to be somewhat chaotic at times as we weave this distinguishable trail like spaghetti on a map. Fortunately Our Heavenly Father is able to track our progress as well as our detours and somehow work out all the details that return us to our purpose and calling. The interactions with others may approach infinity but like a giant jigsaw puzzle, each piece comes together to produce a beautiful picture in the end.

Are you a disruptor towards mankind? Are you hindering others by impeding their growth or pursuit of their life's goals? Know that Our Heavenly Father will protect "hope" that has been given to each of us and will remove any hindrance in whatever manner is necessary to insure the progression to reality. Any disruption will be removed by the most effective means necessary even though it will probably differ from our expectation. In the Scripture, Paul was just such a hindrance. Jesus appeared to him on the road to Damascus and had a corrective interview with Paul who then repented and ended up writing two thirds of the New Testament. Can you imagine the relief of the Christians who were in the cross hairs of Paul's persecution at the time? He had officiated over Stephen's stoning and death and his zeal against Christians was well known. Our Heavenly Father had prepared Paul to spread the Gospel with a full understanding of Old Testament Law. This enabled Paul to compare the Old and the New Testaments thus providing a progressive understanding for the Jews to embrace Our Messiah.

Paul's conversion is a testimony to anyone who thinks he is too far gone to be of service to Our Heavenly Father. Saul (who became Paul) was executing Christians. Does it get any worse than that? Yet Paul ended up being one of the greatest servants of Our Lord Jesus Christ! He went through many trials and tribulations in his missionary journeys but the results were remarkable. He deserved death for his prior deeds but the mercy of Our Heavenly Father prevailed although it did not eliminate judgment all together. There is a price to pay for sin, but the severity was reduced due to Stephen's prayer (on behalf of Paul) just before he was taken up to Heaven at his stoning.

The greatest aspect of hope is that of eternity. When a person receives hope from above, then the fear of death departs. We are eternal beings and will live beyond these fleshly bodies. When Jesus was raised from the dead and appeared to many people afterward throughout the ages, the hope was manifested and the door was opened for our redemption unto Our Heavenly Father. Scripture speaks of a culmination of the age, a new millennium of rest. Just prior to that, there will be turmoil around the globe but we are to fear not and are to place our hope in those words of Jesus:

Luke 21:25-28:

25 "And there will be signs in the sun, in the moon, and in the stars; and on the earth distress of nations, with perplexity, the sea and the waves roaring;

26 "men's hearts failing them from fear and the expectation of those things which are coming on the earth, for the powers of the heavens will be shaken.

27 "Then they will see the Son of Man coming in a cloud with power and great glory.

28 "Now when these things begin to happen, look up and lift up your heads, because your redemption draws near."

Chapter 15

LOVE ENDURES ALL THINGS

*E*ndurance is the power to withstand hardship and stress. Love will remain after all the hardships and challenges of life present themselves to each of us. Typically in the Old Testament when you see the word endure, it is linked to the terms forever and mercy. Mercy is an act of Love and operates in the same realm of eternity as does Love.

Everyone wants the blessings mentioned in Scripture whether those blessings are spiritual, physical, emotional, or financial. Often the problem in lawfully attaining those blessings is one of endurance. No man can really believe that he is going to be rewarded with a blessing when he is in sin but there are many promises in Scripture that are given to us to seek after as we purpose to live according to Our Heavenly Father's will. Does any father want his children to suffer? No!

Endurance is all about maturing and maturing requires stress being applied to strengthen the individual so they can perform in their gifts and calling. If you are called to be a world class swimmer, you cannot simply jump in a pool and break the world record with just your raw talent. Immature talent is no different than no talent at all if it is not developed. We are given innumerable examples of this reality. Each of our muscles requires hardship and stress to grow. Sitting, crawling, standing, and walking are all designed to increase the strength of a baby. Day by day that baby continues to strengthen all of its muscles so that it can progress to the next level of mobility. We all marvel at the progress of a young child yet we generally don't appreciate what is at work from the child's perspective. Each step is filled with hardship and stress as well as uncertainty. From the time we are born, endurance is a part of our lives.

Our emotions will attempt to deter us from our growth into mature Christians. Each of us tends to have an immediate protection-type response when we are faced with adversity whether it be physical, mental, or spiritual. Exercise is a great example. It takes a lot of discipline and motivation to continue an exercise program. Emotionally, we would rather turn over in our comfortable bed and blow off today's exercise regimen. Exercise creates fatigue, sometimes pain, and as we push ourselves, we may test our limit which is counterintuitive to our emotional state. Rest and relaxation satisfy our emotional state. However, slothfulness may result from an overindulgence of relaxation, one of the seven sins mentioned in Proverbs.

Enduring adversity is when it becomes critical to hear the voice of Our Heavenly Father. Is what we are enduring part of our walk to achieve our calling or is it due to a detour we have taken where we will have no blessing and fruitfulness? Starting a winery in a dry climate is asking for pain and an extreme use of resources to achieve any success. When we are experiencing pain or extreme resistance we must ask ourselves these questions. Yes, we will have tests and trials to endure and produce maturity in our lives but we must discern the difference in a test and a detour we've chosen for fleshly reasons. In the big picture, even those detours will produce the mature overcomer we all want to be.

Our family members can be the source of some of our greatest endurance tests. For parents, it tends to be one of the children. For children, it tends to be one of the aged parents. Isn't life wonderful! We are all looking for that Utopia where there are no problems, no tests, and no challenges. Our ego wants us to become wealthy so we can remove all the daily pressures that would challenge us. What would happen if there were no pressures or challenges in life? We would get bored and would go find something to conquer or we would just deteriorate. Most retirees know that you can only play so much golf or card games. Boredom of the familiar soon creeps in and causes us to want a more productive life.

"What should I be doing to further the Kingdom of GOD?" is the question each of us should ask Our Heavenly Father. The answer to this question will produce fulfillment and excitement that we are consciously participating in the big picture. It will give us purpose as we walk out our daily lives. Positively impacting other peoples' lives is what this life is all about. Whether it be your next door neighbor or the waiter at the local restaurant, you can spread love and make their lives of enduring challenges just a little more pleasant. A simple smile or a "thank you" might just be the tipping point in that person's life. Their challenges may be moving them toward despair. They may be thinking that nobody cares about them or the life. Just as a drink of cool water provides the runner with relief after a marathon, an act of kindness can have the same effect on a person caught in the depths of despair.

James 1:12: Blessed [is] the man that endureth temptation: for when he is tried, he shall receive the crown of life, which the Lord hath promised to them that love him (KJV)

Temptation is the trial of our fidelity, integrity, virtue, and constancy. Temptation's goal is to separate us from fellowship with Our Heavenly Father by entering into sin. Each of us is hardwired to procreate, to populate the earth. We were given reproductive organs for this very purpose. However, our ego would have us be led by this urge in an unabated fashion. How many men and women are equipped to raise a couple of dozen kids? The long term impact of submitting to this urge would be disastrous. In HIS Wisdom, Our Heavenly Father provided us direction in handling those fleshly urges, not because HE wanted to punish us, but to look out for our long term best interests. HE wants us to multiply but also to be responsible once our little blessings arrive.

Temptation and fear are closely connected. When a man seeks to fulfill lustful desires, he often has the fear of being incomplete and undesirable at the core of his being. By fulfilling the base sexual desire, he temporarily satisfies this fear. However, when this temporary satisfaction subsides, the fear becomes a little stronger and urge becomes greater. When left unchecked, men resort to those lustful actions that lead to death and destruction. We must endure and resist those temptations that promise us fulfillment only to leave us in worse shape than before. Remember, Our Heavenly Father does not tempt us but calls us to endure temptations that we might be blessed.

Blessing and enduring go hand in hand. When we endure all those temptations, we are rewarded with a "Crown of Life". A crown signifies authority and when we endure, we are given authority over life, a reward of an overcomer, a son of GOD. Just as Jesus endured all the temptations of mankind and brought forth eternal life, we can obtain that same eternal life by HIS blood and walking out the Love life through HIS example.

It won't be easy! Each of us will have our daily skirmishes. Those people with greater callings will have greater mountains to climb as they are being prepared. The trials and testing correspond to the calling and we should keep that in mind while we are in the midst of the battle. The Psalms will comfort us as we are being tried for the Psalmist wrote those words to reassure us that our trial was not unique and unbearable. We must draw on that inner strength of Love to reassure us that soon the trial will be over and the pressure will subside. At times each of us may feel lonely and isolated as we are walking out the endurance test, but we must hold on to the reality of Love and know that Our Heavenly Father is our shield and protector.

Maturity and stamina are the result of enduring all things. Each time we are presented with a trial or test, we grow in maturity. After we fight the battle, each of us should take a moment to reflect on the situation. We should let the emotion die down since most of us get "worked up" and would have a skewed view of the events that took place. In our review of the trial or test, there are many questions to ask? What did Our Heavenly Father reveal to us about ourselves? Did we respond in Love, hate, or revenge? Did we judge others with a righteous judgment or carnal judgment? Did our emotions overpower that "still small voice"? Is there anybody who should receive an apology for our actions? By conducting a critical review of our trials and tests, we gain maturity and revelation that will benefit us in our calling. Just as a runner times his event, we must account for our progress. If we respond in the same immature manner each time we are confronted with a trial, our calling will be put on hold until we grow out of the acts of childishness. Love is constant but everything else in constantly changing, either growing or decaying. If you fail to learn from your trials and tests, you will ultimately experience decay. It may be slow but be assured; the decay will creep up on you like a frog placed in the water over a fire on the stove. One day you will wake up to boiling water and wonder why you are in the predicament you're in. Failure to review these trials is simply an attempt to conceal a cycle of decay and until you reveal this decay, you will not grow.

Love always seeks improvement in life and improvement requires endurance. Anyone who has built a house knows endurance. From the day you break ground, endurance and patience are required as you work with subcontractors during every step of the process. Many adverse factors will arise: weather, unreliable people, materials shortages, etc. Adversity is not a license to judge, but to discern. Throughout the project you are always hoping for perfection only to find "excellence" is the true target. Every board, brick and pipe contains imperfections but when joined together, they are still able to create beauty.

The passage of time and fruitfulness are the measurements of endurance. We are told that as we pursue this Love walk as Jesus did, we will suffer persecution:

2 Timothy 3:

12 Yes, and all who desire to live godly in Christ Jesus will suffer persecution.

13 But evil men and impostors will grow worse and worse, deceiving and being deceived.

14 But you must continue in the things which you have learned and been assured of, knowing from whom you have learned them,

15 and that from childhood you have known the Holy Scriptures, which are able to make you wise for salvation through faith which is in Christ Jesus.

16 All Scripture is given by inspiration of God, and is profitable for doctrine, for reproof, for correction, for instruction in righteousness,

17 that the man of God may be complete, thoroughly equipped for every good work. (NKJV)

The deception of men will promote this test of endurance. They will not listen to reason and will argue an indefensible position only to storm out of the room when they find that confronting righteousness is to no avail. They will regroup in their attempt to extract life from you and will appeal to your compassion and mercy only in attempt to sustain their lawlessness. In those times of confrontation you must return to Scripture and be built up in Love and righteousness with the reassurance that you must stand against this lawlessness that would prevail if you succumb to the deceit that is constantly testing your very core of understanding and revelation. Deception will continue to flourish until the fullness of its time. As it permeates various aspects of society, Love will confront this widespread deception to reveal it as well as to convert those who were snared by its insidious tentacles.

By its very nature, Love ultimately endures to victory. Its patience and endurance will outlast any foe and ultimately convert the foe to a beloved brother. Sometimes this endurance may take the form of "tough" Love. Other times it may minister from a distance to allow the person to experience utter failure. In the parable of the prodigal son, the story is as much about the father as it is about the son. When the son wanted his inheritance, the father knew the outcome of giving the immature, blinded son his inheritance. The son wanted worldly possessions rather than a relationship with his father. Only until he reached an emotional and spiritual low did he come to his senses. His father did love him but found it necessary to love him from a distance. Any of us who are fathers knows the pain that the father went through as his son left his presence preferring the worldly life over a close relationship. The son's immaturity had to be dealt with; he had to fail. In the depths of despair did the son finally see the father's Love. The father endured while the son was walking out this deception. When the son returned, the father rejoiced with a celebration.

The Scripture provides many examples of endurance. From Abraham to Jacob, from Moses to Joshua, from King David to King Jesus, each had to endure hardship, persecution, and temptation before they would complete their calling. Each predecessor to Jesus would prophetically point to His calling. Jesus knew his calling but also understood the endurance test that was set before him. He had to suffer the same things all of us do in order to be that perfect and acceptable sacrifice. He had to endure every challenge equal to or greater than those set before us. This is why only HE is our example to look at when we are in our deepest despair. He provides that cool drink of water when we can no longer sustain ourselves. He vowed to never leave us or forsake us no matter where we find ourselves. The whole world may turn against us but He is only a whisper away and will walk through the trials with us to victory. Love endures all things.

Chapter 16

LOVE NEVER FAILS

*T*he summation of all the previous characteristics of Love is that Love never fails but will overcome each challenge, attain victory over every trial, and restore all relationships resulting in division. Man would have us believe that we are subject to some low level law of nature, political system, or economic system. But instead, we are subject to the Love of Our Heavenly Father whom we were made in His likeness. Man attempts to manipulate that facts and circumvent the truth with some philosophy based on the bias of one's personal history. When Jesus went to the Cross, Love conquered death and thus reaffirmed to mankind that Love never fails, no not ever!

This power and authority reigns supreme over all matter, all thought, and the entire spiritual realm. Our bodies are subject to Love. How do you think that Jesus was able to raise Lazarus from the dead even while his body "stinketh"? Wasn't it love that multiplied the fishes so that Jesus could feed the five thousand? He was moved with compassion when seeing the multitudes in need. He healed the sick then fed them by multiplying the loaves of bread and fish. Clearly, Jesus had command of the molecules that made up the food and was able to evoke a higher law to satisfy the need He saw. How many of us are operating at that level today? Many have operated in great faith, even in Jesus' day. Many have had great hope but how many have had the same level of Love that Jesus walked in? Of whom can it be said that Jesus "has not seen such Love in all the world"?

Men have been on a quest for the Holy Grail. I would submit to you that the "Holy Grail" is found in our hearts, the Holy of Holies where the presence of Our Heavenly Father dwells. Love is truly the bread of life and the rod of authority. The commandment of Love is the law by which we truly live. All else is secondary. Mankind has majored on the minor and has been blinded until now of where the true power lies. Kingdoms on earth have all been temporary. The Roman Empire was destined to fail just as the current empires built by man will. As the empires crumble some men's hearts will fail as they put their trust in these sand castles. Their riches will cease to have any value. Their perceptions will turn to vapor. Only Love will survive and thrive in the Kingdom to come. For eons, devout men and women have been praying The Lord's Prayer and their focus will manifest the glory of the Most High GOD. All other god's will be removed. Love will guide our footsteps and open the door that will only respond to the Key of David. Usurpers have been attempting to open that door for generations but have been unsuccessful. There were times when despair nearly took hold of the righteous but Our Heavenly Father would send a voice in the wilderness to reassure us that Love is on the way and that our salvation draweth nigh.

No matter what the circumstance, Love has the solution. There is nothing more powerful, there is no greater authority than that which is motivated by Love. The Apostle Paul received this progressive revelation from the time he was changed by his encounter with Jesus. Being credited with writing two thirds of the New Testament under the guidance of the Holy Spirit, Paul saw the power of Love in action. Who better to communicate the power of Love than the one who had previously taken pleasure in the attempted death and destruction of the early Christian church. When officiating over Stephen's stoning and observing the selfless Love of Stephen's prayer on behalf of Paul, the seeds of Love were planted. Just as in the Old Testament where physical death occurred because of sin, the New Testament brought forth death by conversion from the old man to the new man. Saul died on the road to Damascus and Paul arose out of death to become a disciple of Christ and walk in Love.

As our journey throughout this physical life takes us through many challenges, our faith in Our Heavenly Father is meant to grow and mature. Our consciousness of the unseen world should develop and flourish knowing that there is more to life than just cause and effect. As we contemplate all the signs around us that point to the Love of The Father, we will be encouraged that the vastness of infinity is truly superior over the finite, limited world we can see. Though the concept of infinity may be introduced to us in a math class in high school, or a sermon on the immensity of the universe, or even the unending questions of a four year old, our introduction into the vast unknown will spark our consciousness in knowing that there is a great and powerful Supreme Being that has knowingly created all of this order in the universe. The intent of Our Creator evoked a compression of unfathomable magnitude and the elements of our atomic chart were born. Scientists have identified a "big bang" that took place but have yet to explain the prior compression that was required to release the energy necessary for the big bang in the first place. Expansion is preceded by compression and compression is preceded by intent. We will ultimately conclude that this intent was communicated by Our Heavenly Father's Love.

Everything in the universe has a unique electromagnetic signature. Those protons, neutrons, and electrons combined with all of those "GOD" particles at the subatomic level give off a unique signal. What causes the unending spin of the electrons around the nucleus? Magnetism you say? What causes magnetism? As we drill down deeper and deeper into the smallest common denominator of subatomic observation, we will ultimately affirm that Love consciousness is the "glue" that holds all of creation together.

All of us are at different stages or levels of consciousness and understanding. Some of us are downright blinded to the understanding of Love. Some of us are in the midst of life- threatening turmoil. Others are at peace or possibly recovering from some skirmish in the journey of life. Yet others are living an uneventful existing wondering what is the meaning or purpose of their lives. There are those in temporary control and others in temporary subjection to that control. I use the word "temporary" because the control by one man over another is not indefinite for Love will always promote truth and that truth will set you free. Truth has its foundation in Love and will always promote growth whereas control is always subject to decay. Man was not created to be a slave to another man. Religions have been created to promote control over the populations only to find that as men look up toward the heavens, they come to realize that control misappropriates the law in favor of a few at the expense of many. "Suddenly" people wake up to the reality of control and no longer accept the responsibility to provide others in control with all of the benefits of life. Lust takes, whereas Love gives.

We take the laws of physics for granted as we unknowingly expect the law of gravity to work every second of every single day. Can you imagine life without gravity? Love's intent is all around us waiting to be discovered as we stop our busy lives and just take time to be quiet and contemplate all of the mysteries around us. Consider the hummingbird that should not be able to fly or the child who begins to learn the language of its parents, one word at a time. Life is shouting Love all around us if we would only have eyes to see!

With 1% of the universe visible and 99% invisible, we must turn our attention to what we call the intangible aspects of life. We have been majoring on the minor. What if we realized that the next age of earth was going to be ushered in by the consciousness of Love among a notable group of people? What if Our Heavenly Father has been exposing our consciousness to that fact so that we would embrace Love and begin to sing a Heavenly song that would prophetically call forth the final age of "Love"? The prophets of old called forth hope and the prophets of recent centuries have ushered in faith. Isn't now time for the greatest virtue to become the basis of our society? Imagine a government where we had true public servants. Think about how our lives would change for the better as we no longer had to be concerned about the exploitation of the weak. Peace among men would prevail as the standard, not the exception. A synergistic effect would cause resources to be distributed so that all men could flourish rather than a few who controlled those resources in that past. Excesses in one area would meet the needs of other areas. Equilibrium would be achieved by Love prevailing on the earth.

As we become motivated by Love, new discoveries will unlock the storehouses of Heaven. Just as Jesus healed the sick, those who walk in Love will remove the need of inefficient medical practice as well as all of the toxic chemicals currently used to manage physical pain. We will appreciate the supernatural after having been subjected to the current system. Jesus was never limited by the seen but operated in both realms as the need arose. Some of us have observed incidents of this unseen realm by being exposed to miracles superseding the natural course of events. When the supernatural occurs, man is drawn to the event in awe. Deep down inside we are "wired" to expect the supernatural to arrive. Our quest to discover solutions to our current problems will result in the expansion of our consciousness. Only Our Heavenly

Father knows the point when widespread manifestation of this consciousness will occur. Innumerable prayers that His Kingdom come on earth will soon be answered.

Love produces true growth, creativity, production, decency, and innocence. Men will discover the power of truth and how it facilitates growth and productivity. Honesty prevails where men honor the truth and truth brings clarity and certainty to our understanding of reality. Reality operates in all realms and as we honor truth, we open ourselves up to the revelation of the unseen. Think not that men without Love will be able to take control of the unseen and dominate the masses as they have managed to do in the physical, seen world. This unseen world promises to reward those who truly seek this life of Love that has been described in this writing. As for me and my family, we will set our focus on this walk of Love and become more like the character of Our Heavenly Father. Will we encounter resistance? Absolutely! At a personal level, our egos will fight to keep in control but only to find out there is no way to overcome Love. Knowing this, it is just a matter of time before our egos will submit to the command of Love in our hearts and we begin to operate in the arena of the unseen. Just as the Baptism of the Holy Spirit came down on the people at one location and spread throughout the earth, the Baptism of Love will prove to be even a greater outpouring with even greater manifestations of the supernatural for Love is the source of all miracles. When this change occurs, magnetism will replace force as the fundamental energy source. New relationships will be forged and synchronicity will be found spreading throughout the earth. Effortless simplicity will replace the demands of complexity and forgiveness will wipe away all of the tension separating people over the last centuries

How do I participate in this new millennium? I suspect that the mere fact you have read this means that there is a force drawing you to this revelation of Love. That attraction will continue to move you away from judgment and toward reconciliation of all things. May that Light whose seeds of Love are planted in you, grow and manifest for all to see! Let HIS Kingdom come and HIS Will be done on earth as it is in Heaven...

Part 2:

OTHER FACETS

Chapter 17

LOVE YOUR ENEMIES

One of the greatest challenges to overcome is to "love your enemies". An enemy is an opposing, often hostile, person or group of people. The enemy may attack you by some type of force that challenges your well being or livelihood.

In the Old Testament, Israel had many enemies who attempted to conquer them and some were successful. We are told that Israel's losses were due to some type of corporate sin where their covering was lifted. When they turned away from their relationship with OUR HEAVENLY FATHER, their enemies were able to defeat them. After they repented, they once again became victorious. The following Scripture provides the details of how the LORD dealt with Israel's sin:

2 Samuel 24:11-15:

11 For when David was up in the morning, the word of the LORD came unto the prophet Gad, David's seer, saying,

12 Go and say unto David, Thus saith the LORD, I offer thee three [things]; choose thee one of them, that I may [do it] unto thee.

13 So Gad came to David, and told him, and said unto him, Shall seven years of famine come unto thee in thy land? or wilt thou flee three months before thine enemies, while they pursue thee? or that there be three days' pestilence in thy land? now advise, and see what answer I shall return to him that sent me.

14 And David said unto Gad, I am in a great strait: let us fall now into the hand of the LORD; for his mercies [are] great: and let me not fall into the hand of man.

15 So the LORD sent a pestilence upon Israel from the morning even to the time appointed: and there died of the people from Dan even to Beersheba seventy thousand men.

Until the ministry of Jesus, the mentality of the people was to hate their enemies and ultimately conquer them. When Jesus arrived on the scene, the Jewish leadership was looking for a conquering Messiah and failed to see that Jesus was the promised Messiah. Since Jesus did not meet their requirements of a Messiah, Jesus was their enemy and they were concerned about losing their positions as leaders of the Jewish nation.

Jesus blasted away the doctrine of hate with the following words:

Matthew 5:43-45
43 "You have heard that it was said, 'You shall love your neighbor and hate your enemy.'

44 But I say to you, love your enemies, bless those who curse you, do good to those who hate you, and pray for those who spitefully use you and persecute you, 45 For if you love those who love you, what reward have you? Do not even the tax collectors do the same?

Jesus revealed the real definition of love to the world since their view of love was a conditionally motivated love- "I'll love you if you love me". He revealed to us that love is unconditional and requires nothing from the recipient in order to express itself. Further, love does not depend on a relationship to act. There is no better Scripture to reflect this reality than John 3:16, "For God so loved the world, that he gave his only begotten Son, that whosoever believeth in him should not perish, but have everlasting life." The Apostle Paul explained to us that God's great love initiated our salvation while we were dead in sins:

Ephesians 2:4-9:
4 But God, who is rich in mercy, for his great love wherewith he loved us,
5 Even when we were dead in sins, hath quickened us together with Christ, (by grace ye are saved;)
6 And hath raised [us] up together, and made [us] sit together in heavenly [places] in Christ Jesus:
7 That in the ages to come he might shew the exceeding riches of his grace in [his] kindness toward us through Christ Jesus.

8 For by grace are ye saved through faith; and that not of yourselves: [it is] the gift of God:

9 Not of works, lest any man should boast.

This was an unconditional act of love toward all of mankind. A friend of mine would often say, "If you are to love your friends and you are to love your enemies, who else is there"? In the Old Testament Israel conquered their enemies, in the New Testament we are to convert our enemies. According to Christ, a neighbor is any other man irrespective of nation or religion with whom we live or whom we chance to meet. According to the Jews, a neighbor was a fellow citizen of their nation. Jesus corrected their understanding of the commandment to love thy neighbor by commanding them to "bless those who curse you, do good to those who hate you, and pray for those who spitefully use you and persecute you".

Love is reconciliatory by nature and brings an end to the division created by an enemy. The enemy will use deceit to divide and conquer whereas love will use truth to ultimately bring reconciliation. Why does a division occur? It will occur when one of the parties involved is motivated by something other than love and attempts to compensate for failure by using force or deceit to gain advantage over the other party.

In a lawsuit, the person filing the lawsuit claims the other person took unfair advantage of the claimant or harmed him in some way. If the claimant was hearing the voice of God, how could he claim loss by responding to God's voice? If this person was put into the situation where the loss occurred, he either did not hear the voice of God or, Our Heavenly Father placed him into divine judgment ultimately to teach him a lesson and restore his relationship with Our Heavenly Father.

Paul, in 1 Corinthians 6, wrote "If any of you has a dispute with another, dare he take it before the ungodly for judgment instead of before the saints?" If a dispute arises, we are to take it before those who can hear the voice of The Lord rather than the worldly system which is based on traditions of man, manipulation, and deceit. How often have we heard of the best lawyer winning rather than the truth prevailing?

"Thou shalt not bear false witness" requires us to be truthful about our relationship with others. Manipulation of the facts has no part in this commandment. Manipulation is an insidious characteristic of our society today and it has infiltrated nearly every aspect of commerce as well as personal relationships. Manipulation is an attempt to control the person, situation, or outcome. It will exploit the weakness of the other party to gain a dominant position in a situation. Misuse of your God given talents frequently results in manipulation. Lusting after or coveting someone else's property or calling promotes manipulation and if taken to an extreme will create an enemy "deserving to be conquered". If someone else has something you are lusting after, you find a flaw or weakness in them and turn the focus on that flaw or weakness, exploit it, then rationalize why you deserve to remove the thing you are lusting after. Isn't that process at the root of adultery?

Consider what would happen if society was motivated by love? How many laws would we need? Just one, as Paul wrote:

Galatians 5:14: For all the law is fulfilled in one word, [even] in this; Thou shalt love thy neighbour as thyself.

If our every action was motivated by love, there would be no conflict or dispute to settle in court, civil or criminal. Love serves your neighbor rather than exploiting some weakness to extract something from that person. Romans 13:10 tells us that " Love worketh no ill to his neighbour: therefore love [is] the fulfilling of the law." Troublesome, injurious, pernicious, or destructive behavior is no longer found among those who walk in love. Our motivation would move from self-centeredness to blessing our neighbor with our gifts and calling. What a world this would be!

What happens if your enemy forces you into a battle? Your responsibility is to end it as effectively as possible, in love. Your stand must be based on truth and facts, not emotion and perceptions. Often people who force a battle with someone walking in love are doing so in a blinded manner. They are being led by their egos and idols in their hearts thus all of their actions center around the fulfillment of the idols in their hearts. Their prayers will be answered according to those idols and perpetuate their calamity. Does The Lord answer in this fashion? Yes! Ezekiel 14:4 reveals this:

"Therefore speak unto them, and say unto them, Thus saith the Lord GOD; Every man of the house of Israel that setteth up his idols in his heart, and putteth the stumblingblock of his iniquity before his face, and cometh to the prophet; I the LORD will answer him that cometh according to the multitude of his idols;" (KJV)

"I the LORD will answer him that cometh according to the multitude of his idols" means exactly what it says. Those with idols in their hearts are on a path towards destruction and that path may lead to an "early" departure from the physical body- death. I have witnessed this situation multiple times where individuals have impeded the ministry of another in order to fulfill their own agenda. Frequently those people die of either a heart attack or cancer. A close friend of mine is a retired oncologist (cancer doctor) and practiced medicine for forty years. It was his custom to pray for his patients. There were times when The Lord would tell him that his prayers for the patient's recovery would be of none effect, the patient's illness was do to a spiritual problem. The patient would soon die. Our society has attempted to disengage physical health from spiritual health, WRONG! As you pursue a path of being an enemy to someone else, you put your own future at risk as well as those you have a covenant with.

How do I know if I have idols in my heart? Ask Our Heavenly Father to reveal them to you and repent immediately. His Great Grace and Mercy motivated by His Love will respond to your request but beware, it might be ugly.

When you judge a person or matter based on the idols in your heart, you will surely make the wrong decision or take the wrong action. Jesus warned us of this type of judgment:

Matthew 7:1-6:

"JUDGE not, that you be not judged.

"For with what judgment you judge, you will be judged; and with the measure you use, it will be measured back to you.

"And why do you look at the speck in your brother's eye, but do not consider the plank in your own eye?

"Or how can you say to your brother, 'Let me remove the speck from your eye'; and look, a plank is in your own eye?

"Hypocrite! First remove the plank from your own eye, and then you will see clearly to remove the speck from your brother's eye.

"Do not give what is holy to the dogs; nor cast your pearls before swine, lest they trample them under their feet, and turn and tear you in pieces. (NKJV)

As those great and profound words have echoed, "We have found the enemy, and the enemy is us". (POGO, the cartoon)

What are we to do about those enemies who want to do us harm? Contrary to what the world would advise, Jesus tells us what to do:

Matthew 5:44: But I say unto you, Love your enemies, bless them that curse you, do good to them that hate you, and pray for them which despitefully use you, and persecute you; (KJV)

The flesh wants to lash out at the enemy, the ego wants to dominate the enemy, and our survival instinct wants to eliminate the enemy by force. Jesus tells us those actions are wrong. Before the arrival of the revelation of Love (Jesus), people died from their sin. In the New Testament people are converted. Thus we need to practice the words of Jesus over our enemies:

- Love your enemy
- Bless them that curse you
- Do good to them that hate you
- Pray for them which despitefully use you
- Pray for them that persecute you

What will our reward be for joyfully following these commands? You will then be perfect, complete, and mature in Christ and you will also recognize your intimate relationship with Our Heavenly Father.

As we focus our actions on the above steps, we proceed on a new, vibrant path of Love. It may seem uneventful at first. Just as it is when you begin a long trip, the closer you are to your destination, the more distinct is the change of scenery. It has been said that "success breeds success" but I can tell you "Love produces more Love".

Chapter 18

LOVE UNIFIES

John 10:30: I and [my] Father are one. (KJV)

Is there a greater statement in Scripture than this one? Jesus proclaimed the fullness of His relationship with Our Heavenly Father to the Jews on Solomon's porch at the Temple. Rather than rejoice, they picked up stones to kill him but were not able to carry out their intent.

Any action or thought that causes dissension, separation, or isolation is not motivated out of love. Love promotes restoration and reconciliation for that was the mission of Jesus—to reconcile and restore mankind to Our Heavenly Father.

The earth was formed and framed with unity. GOD created the heavens and earth and established all of the physical laws governing physical existence. Stars, planets, structures, molecules, atoms, protons, neutrons, electrons, and sub-atomic particles all operate by magnetism. There is a fundamental attraction to a unified state in all physical matter. We totally rely on this natural law for our very existence. What would happen if this law were to suddenly change?

Unity is the source of intelligence. Without unity there would be no communication to transfer information between to parties and without this transfer, no priorities in life could be established. One of the more dramatic examples of unity came early in Scripture.

Genesis 11:1-9:

1 And the whole earth was of one language, and of one speech.

2 And it came to pass, as they journeyed from the east, that they found a plain in the land of Shinar; and they dwelt there.

3 And they said one to another, Go to, let us make brick, and burn them thoroughly. And they had brick for stone, and slime had they for mortar.

4 And they said, Go to, let us build us a city and a tower, whose top [may reach] unto heaven; and let us make us a name, lest we be scattered abroad upon the face of the whole earth.

5 And the LORD came down to see the city and the tower, which the children of men builded.

6 And the LORD said, Behold, the people [is] one, and they have all one

language; and this they begin to do: and now nothing will be restrained from them, which they have imagined to do.

7 Go to, let us go down, and there confound their language, that they may not understand one another's speech.

8 So the LORD scattered them abroad from thence upon the face of all the earth: and they left off to build the city.

9 Therefore is the name of it called Babel; because the LORD did there confound the language of all the earth: and from thence did the LORD scatter them abroad upon the face of all the earth.

The Tower of Babel illustrates what man can do when he is in one accord with his fellow man. The LORD stated in verse 6 that nothing is impossible for those who are operating as "one". The problem with this population was that they were attempting to exalt themselves rather than serving one another thus they had to be stopped from their unrighteous behavior. Confounding their communication and scattering them abroad was the answer. However, if they had been operating in love, they would have brought heaven to earth. Unity and communication brings forth a power that is so great that it must be protected from perversion at all cost even to the point of direct intervention by The Lord of Hosts.

Unity in Love is the key to solving the world's problems. This untapped power awaits those who would seek its fulfillment by initiating and pursuing love each and every day. As more join in, I expect this power and authority will increase exponentially throughout the earth. Solutions to the world's problems will proceed forth from Heaven to those who are qualified to steward the solutions. Our Heavenly Father will protect the solutions from those wolves in sheep's clothing. Surely He will scatter those who would attempt to thwart those who are operating in Love and are called to bring forth peace.

Love properly defines your priorities in life. What should you do with your time? By following Love, you get the most "bang for the buck". Jesus did not minister healing to everyone He encountered. How did He determine His priorities?

John 5:30: I can of mine own self do nothing: as I hear, I judge: and my judgment is just; because I seek not mine own will, but the will of the Father which hath sent me. (KJV)

Jesus spent time in communion with Our Heavenly Father. How would you like to knowingly spend each day as directed by The Lord? Awareness is the beginning of that path. The purpose of this book is to make you aware of the fullness of Love that awaits you as you pursue the path of Love. Jesus clearly explains the effectiveness of His life by revealing His fulfilling relationship with Our Heavenly Father. Who else in a mere 42 months has had such an impact on this earth over the last 2,000 years? Awareness occurs without the assistance of the mind's logic and is a prior event. Our Heavenly Father makes us aware of a revelation by various means allowing us to pursue that revelation thus giving us the opportunity to expand our knowledge and understanding as a precursor to acting on the revelation. In short, He opens our eyes and ears (or closes them):

Deuteronomy 29:4: Yet the LORD hath not given you an heart to perceive, and eyes to see, and ears to hear, unto this day. (KJV)

In protecting His plan of Love, The LORD restricts perceiving, seeing, and hearing thus you are not aware of the potential of change until you turn away from your wicked ways. When you repent of the direction which moves you away from your calling, you provide the basis by which you can begin to perceive, hear, and see your purpose that was established before you entered the womb. This begins a process of purification of the heart from all of the acts and thoughts that caused the separation from your Heavenly Father. As you are cleansed of the uncleanness, your awareness increases and you begin to hear that still small voice. Ask the Father to remove the impurities in your heart. Ask the Father to show you those people whom you need to ask forgiveness. Purity comes from cleansing and removing all of those little specks that have entered in. A new world awaits you as Jesus said:

Matthew 5:8: Blessed [are] the pure in heart: for they shall see God. (KJV)

A specific characteristic of unity is exchange and there is some form of communication which occurs as two become in unity with each other. This unity brings forth intelligence and revelation with it. Jesus showed us of the ability to be one with The Father and we saw the fruit of it in His life. The whole is greater than the some of the parts. As we become one with Our Heavenly Father, new doors will open to us. We will tap a previously undiscovered and unlimited resource allowing us to fulfill our purpose and destiny as children of GOD. Unity is a sacred aspect of the equation as we see in the following:

Mark 10:6-9:

6 "But from the beginning of the creation, God 'made them male and female.'

7 'For this reason a man shall leave his father and mother and be joined to his wife,

8 'and the two shall become one flesh'; so then they are no longer two, but one flesh.

9 "Therefore what God has joined together, let not man separate."

Marriage is a primary form of unity. It provides us an excellent example of unity and expresses the nature of relationship between GOD and man. Jesus is referred to as the groom and the church or body of believers represents the bride of Christ. This union is meant to be unbroken, the ultimate unity. For unity to occur the two must first become aware of each other. Afterwards, communication begins. As communication occurs, the connection is established and begins to nourish each other and in turn growth occurs. As Paul wrote:

Ephesians 4:16: From whom the whole body fitly joined together and compacted by that which every joint supplieth, according to the effectual working in the measure of every part, maketh increase of the body unto the edifying of itself in love. (KJV)

When the whole body of Christ has come together where each person is operating according to his purpose (being fitted), the body of Christ is held together by what every person supplies. Each person must be "properly working" to cause growth of the body of Christ, for the building up of itself in love. This is what Paul meant by the "perfecting of the saints". The emphasis is supplying or serving rather than receiving. Receiving is the result of supplying, not the opposite.

What seeds are you sowing: unity or separation? Any person, family, community, city, state, country, or civilization that sows the seeds of separation will fail just as Jesus said "any house divided against itself, shall not stand".

What can we do to promote unity?

• Communicate with each other for no unity will occur without exchange

• Grow up, put away those childish characteristics of selfishness.

• Write a letter to someone telling them how much they mean to you. Emails and text messages don't count. Take some quality time.

• Do an act of service for someone you know

• Smile, a simple form of communication

Chapter 19

SELF SERVING MOTIVATION

*M*an's carnal nature promotes judgment. Everything and everybody goes through a "judgment" filter. In subtleness, people look for flaws and weaknesses in others and by doing this the person perceives that they are in control.

Mat 5:43-46: "Ye have heard that it hath been said, Thou shalt love thy neighbour, and hate thine enemy. But I say unto you, Love your enemies, bless them that curse you, do good to them that hate you, and pray for them which despitefully use you, and persecute you; That ye may be the children of your Father which is in heaven: for he maketh his sun to rise on the evil and on the good, and sendeth rain on the just and on the unjust. For if ye love them which love you, what reward have ye? do not even the publicans the same? And if ye salute your brethren only, what do ye more [than others]? do not even the publicans so? Be ye therefore perfect, even as your Father which is in heaven is perfect."

As Jesus told us, we are to love everybody and therefore we should be careful to judge no one. Scarcity in our life fuels the self serving attitude. When we judge somebody else we must look within ourselves to see why that attitude exists. Our ego wants to defend the thoughts or words spoken in an effort to justify the scarcity that exists within us. This internal flaw must be isolated and dug out of our soul that we may have no hindrance as we seek to fellowship with Our Heavenly Father.

Have you ever wondered why you can't seem to get a break in an area important to you? You need not look any further than the mirror. You have either taken a path that is not part of your calling or you have some issue that is preventing one or more of your gifts from operating properly. Our Heavenly Father does not hold you back because He simply wants to see you fail! He only wants the best result for you.

1 John 2:15-16:
15 Do not love the world or the things in the world. If anyone loves the world, the love of the Father is not in him.
16 For all that is in the world--the lust of the flesh, the lust of the eyes, and the pride of life--is not of the Father but is of the world. (NKJV)

In most cases the self serving motivation may be placed in one of the three categories mentioned in the above Scripture. Since money is the primary medium to attain what we do not have, we are warned against focusing our love on money. Men can seek to satisfy their lust of the flesh by purchasing time of a prostitute. They can "bribe" beautiful women by showering them with expensive gifts to make them feel special. Men can appear to give generously to universities or church campuses in order to have a building named after them so that they will be exalted even after death. Since money is a medium for any exchange men have found that if they focus on acquiring money, they can feed their lusts in a much easier manner. Jesus warned against this pursuit:

Mark 10:25: It is easier for a camel to go through the eye of a needle, than for a rich man to enter into the kingdom of God. (KJV)

Since the root word of "needle" is associated with a sharp object, we know Jesus literally meant a sewing needle, not a small gate requiring a camel to get on its knees to enter in. The question becomes: "Do you have riches or, do riches have you?" The disciples were amazed at His statement.

Mark 10:26: And they were astonished out of measure, saying among themselves, Who then can be saved? (KJV)

Obviously there was a conflict surfacing here. The blessings of Our Heavenly Father include wealth, for many of the promises given in the Old Testament were blessing of fruitfulness and wealth. How can on one hand Our Heavenly Father provide us money and on the other hand have His Most Holy Son make the above statement? The key resides in your priorities. Are you willing to give when Our Heavenly Father requests it? Wealthy people in their self-serving motivation will give a notable amount of money but as a percentage of their wealth, it is small. In the story of the widow's mite, we are shown that Our Heavenly Father looks at the percentage of wealth you are giving, not the amount.

To some degree, money represents our life. If I make ten dollars per hour, then ten dollars represent one hour of that portion of my life devoted to work on this earth. If I give one thousand dollars to minister to the need of a widow, the gift represents 100 working hours to me. However if I receive $125 per hour, then I have given an equivalent of one 8 hour workday of my life to help another. Who gave more to the widow?

In today's current system, wealth is power. I have seen men become like immature children seeking attention when in the midst of an extremely wealthy man. Each man attempts to show himself as something special so that he may gain favor by the rich man in hopes of tapping into some of that wealth. It matters not how the wealth was obtained whether by hook or crook. Men simply want more money in attempt to satisfy their lusts. By focusing our attention on Our Heavenly Father and not on money, we open ourselves up to blessings, including money. When we start looking at money as a tool of the Kingdom rather than a means of satisfying a lust then we are on the road to blessings from above. We must keep our focus on Heaven above for the wealth in this world is a slippery road to destruction.

Feeding our lusts is like the proverbial boiling of the frog in water. We start out rationalizing how the lustful act did not reap any consequences and thus it may not have been a lustful act after all. Before long, we seek a sign which acts as an affirmation that our lustful act is really part of our destiny and should be embraced. But can we be sure? We seek additional self-serving signs and they show up as expected and we are now steeped in the lust separating ourselves from our relationship with Our Heavenly Father as well as our calling. Using and interpreting signs can be hazardous to your health:

Matthew 16:4: A wicked and adulterous generation seeketh after a sign; and there shall no sign be given unto it, but the sign of the prophet Jonas. And he left them, and departed. (KJV)

Jesus made it quite clear that a wicked and adulterous people seek a sign of justification and/or revelation. Signs are important but moreover interpretation of signs is critical. The Scripture is full of signs, parables, prophecies, and predictions but you need the Holy Spirit to interpret the meanings in order to insure you will not be misled by man or your own ego. I asked Our Heavenly Father about signs and He said, "All signs originate with me but not all of them are applicable to you". Signs are not to be used as our primary motivator but should only be used as a confirmation of what Our Heavenly Father has spoken to us.

Matthew 16:3: And in the morning, [It will be] foul weather to day: for the sky is red and lowering. O [ye] hypocrites, ye can discern the face of the sky; but can ye not [discern] the signs of the times? (KJV)

In the above Scripture, there are two types of "discerning". The hypocrites can mentally interpret the weather by previous experience whereas they are unable to spiritually discern a sign transcending the course of nature.

Don't get me wrong, signs of confirmation given by Our Heavenly Father are great! When we are a little shaky in our walk, Our Heavenly Father nudges us with needed confirmations of encouragement. However, we must be vigilant in our submission to signs and not use them to initiate action but only to confirm what we hear from Our Heavenly Father.

In the Parable of the Sower, Jesus not only speaks the parable but interprets it for His disciples. This parable is about fruitfulness and the hindrances to fruitfulness. The Christian must be careful when hearing the Word of GOD for he will receive it with gladness but that is only one part of the equation. The condition of his heart will determine whether good fruit is produced and multiplied:

Mark 4:19 "and the cares of this world, the deceitfulness of riches, and the desires for other things entering in choke the word, and it becomes unfruitful. (NKJV)

Care, riches, and lusts will cause you to be unfruitful. What can we do to prevent the Word from being choked out of our hearts? Love your fellow man instead of considering ways to extract his assets or take his wife. Simplify your life and consider those things you just couldn't live without that sit in your house or garage gathering dust. Stop and listen, dwell and meditate on the Word of GOD. Downsize your "needs" and de-clutter your life and you will suddenly have less cares of the world, riches will lose their influence on you, and "things" will no longer entice you to be drawn away.

It's time to do a self-analysis of whether or not your ego has you walking out a self-serving life:

Do you tell your boss about your various unexpected financial woes? Aren't you really making him or her feel guilty that you need a raise? Don't you know that your Heavenly Father knows your needs if you would only seek His Voice?

When you buy something new, do you shout it from the rooftops hoping to impress everyone? Don't get me wrong, it doesn't hurt to share it with your friends so they can rejoice with you but are you genuinely excited when they acquire something new?

Reflect on what you talk about all day long. Does it center on you or the other person?

As you are speaking to another person, is the topic always about "I"?

Do you consistently get mad when you don't get your way?

Do you find the "negative" in what others say?

When is the last time you did something for another person without expecting something in return?

Have you attempted to reconcile with an enemy?

Are you looking for signs to justify your actions rather asking Our Heavenly Father what actions to take today?

Are you taking Scripture out of context to justify self-serving motivations?

Be honest with yourself. If you are guilty of self serving motivations, change and take action to correct those areas that plague your daily walk. When you wake up in the morning, think of what you can do to tell your ego that it is not in control but you are led by every Word of Our Heavenly Father. Walk the walk!

Your actions can either promote life or death, therefore promote life. Preachers from the pulpit or TV screen have exploited the people beating them over the head with Scripture in order to extract finances from them. I personally know of a family who went bankrupt because of their giving. They were promised blessing only to end up with hungry children and the loss of their home. While the pastor drives around in a luxury car, the people are in lack. How sad is it to see Our Heavenly Father's Words used by self-centered people who claim to represent His Kingdom. Love does not exploit the less fortunate but lifts them up. Love turns the focus from me to thee.

Chapter 20

OUR COVENANT OF LOVE

*D*oes each of us have a covenant with Our Heavenly Father? We sure do and He revealed that fact to Jeremiah:

Jeremiah 1:4-9:
Then the word of the LORD came unto me, saying,

Before I formed thee in the belly I knew thee; and before thou camest forth out of the womb I sanctified thee, [and] I ordained thee a prophet unto the nations.

Then said I, Ah, Lord GOD! behold, I cannot speak: for I [am] a child.

But the LORD said unto me, Say not, I [am] a child: for thou shalt go to all that I shall send thee, and whatsoever I command thee thou shalt speak.

Be not afraid of their faces: for I [am] with thee to deliver thee, saith the LORD.

Then the LORD put forth his hand, and touched my mouth. And the LORD said unto me, Behold, I have put my words in thy mouth. (KJV)

There is a unique and special reason every person was created. Each of us has a purpose in life and this purpose was designed specifically by The Father. With that purpose or calling, we were given gifts specifically required to fulfill our purpose. Jeremiah did not think he had the required gifts for his calling but quickly found out that the gifts laying dormant in him were activated by a "touch" in a moment of time.

Have you ever noticed how children are drawn to specific areas of interest at an early age? Our grandson is enamored with construction equipment and he can spend hours watching cranes at a high rise construction site. One of his early words was "backhoe". Could it be that he is called to construct? As parents, our responsibility is to encourage the child's gifts and calling, whatever it may be. It is not to live out our unfulfilled dreams through the child, the ego is at the source of that action. Let the child pursue their God inspired dream and enjoy the child's development and fulfillment.

What do you do if you don't know your calling? You will need to take some remedial steps which begin with "hearing the Lord". Also, you will need to quit imitating or envying other people.

When I was a child, I would watch Superman on television and then go outside to play with my friends and we would imitate Superman as best as we could. Mom's old white sheets became our capes and fortunately the limbs on the trees were not high enough to cause us injury when we jumped and replicated the flight of the masked crusader. Our imaginations served us well. But when I became a man it was time to put away childish things. "When I was a child, I spake as a child, I understood as a child, I thought as a child: but when I became a man, I put away childish things."(1 Corinthians 13:11) When we imitate others, we begin to idolize them and at the same time we discount our own gifts and callings. We effectively communicate to ourselves and the world is that our individual gifts and calling given to us by Our Heavenly Father is not as meaningful or important as the gifts and calling of the person we are imitating. Hollywood movie makers spend tremendous amounts of money creating a personality out of someone who before they were "discovered" might have been waiting tables.

Where imitation focuses on being the other person, envy tends to focus on wanting or obsessing over the possessions of another person. This can often be found in the extreme when being in the company of a very wealthy person. People flock to this person as though some of his wealth will mystically transfer to them as they align themselves with the wealthy person. Of course the wealthy person encourages this behavior to feed his own ego and support the belief that by his accumulated wealth he has been singled out as being superior or special.

Proverbs 14:30: A sound heart [is] the life of the flesh: but envy the rottenness of the bones. (KJV)

When Howard Hughes, one of the wealthiest men of his time, had passed away, his accountant was asked by a reporter how much money Hughes had left behind. "All of it" was his comment. If we could step back for a moment and truly comprehend the brevity of that statement, we would truly change our view of money, power, fame, and fortune.

Resentment is a feeling of deep and bitter anger and ill-will thus when you add bitterness to envy the result is resentment. People who resent others display their bitterness by disparaging the other person, finding flaws and passing judgment. This allows them to exalt themselves above the targeted person as though by exalting oneself, Our Heavenly Father will wave a magic wand and make it so. When a person is bitter, their soul is not satisfied as Proverbs 27:7 tells us:

"A satisfied soul loathes the honeycomb, But to a hungry soul every bitter thing is sweet."

When we don't know what our covenant with Our Heavenly Father is, we have this insatiable hunger that needs to be fulfilled, we have this need to be completed. Unfortunately many Christian speakers have led us to believe that if we have a call on our life, it must be in the five-fold ministry as stated in Ephesians 4:11. Is the bricklayer who helped build the Temple in Solomon's time any less important to Our Heavenly Father than Solomon himself?

Our Heavenly Father protects our callings. Throughout Scripture we see how men and women were guided through life's challenges, trained in various ways, and received revelation at key times in their lives to prepare them for their calling. In the Old Testament Joseph was a great example.

When Joseph was young (believed to be about 17) he was given a dream by The Lord that his brothers would bow down before him. Of course this is not what the brothers wanted to hear. Joseph was younger and was not in line for the inheritance of Jacob but that did not stop him from sharing his dream. The brothers were outraged by this young, brash kid prophesying something this outrageous. Their egos kicked in and they decided to get rid of Joseph. At first they planned to simply kill him and throw him in a pit for the animals to feast on. Reuben quieted the brothers and they all agreed to sell Joseph to some Ishmeelites came from Gilead on their way to Egypt.

I am sure Joseph was not prepared for this aspect of his covenant with Our Heavenly Father. He was expecting smooth sailing toward the fulfillment of the dream without any of the physical, mental, and emotional challenges that were to come. His road to fulfillment took him to Egypt as a slave. His God given gifts promoted him and men saw that the Hand of The Lord was on him:

Genesis 39:1-5:

1 And Joseph was brought down to Egypt; and Potiphar, an officer of Pharaoh, captain of the guard, an Egyptian, bought him of the hands of the Ishmeelites, which had brought him down thither.

2 And the LORD was with Joseph, and he was a prosperous man; and he was in the house of his master the Egyptian.

3 And his master saw that the LORD [was] with him, and that the LORD made all that he did to prosper in his hand.

4 And Joseph found grace in his sight, and he served him:

and he made him overseer over his house, and all [that] he had he put into his hand.

5 And it came to pass from the time [that] he had made him overseer in his house, and over all that he had, that the LORD blessed the Egyptian's house for Joseph's sake; and the blessing of the LORD was upon all that he had in the house, and in the field. (KJV)

"And that the LORD made all that he did to prosper in his hand" is a great promise to each of us as we pursue our calling. We must know that the LORD will prosper us in our calling and HE will protect us as we pursue the fulfillment of our purpose. HE does not hand out gifts and callings light heartedly. If you had no purpose, he would not have formed you in the womb.

Joseph was in Potiphar's house but still had not fulfilled his calling. He needed some more training and his ego needed to be dealt with. What better place to resolve the ego problem than prison! After all, his ego is what provoked his brothers to sell him as a slave in the first place. So off to prison he went. What happened to the fulfillment of that dream?

As the plan would have it, Joseph's fellow prisoners just happen to have access to Pharaoh and when Pharaoh has a dream that needs interpreted, Joseph is thrust into the limelight. AND SUDDENLY, Joseph becomes second in command over Egypt and finally the stage is set for the fulfillment of the dream. Joseph had plenty of time to ponder his gifts, his calling, and the hindrances to the fulfillment.

By now he knew his immaturity must be dealt with. The ego and that brazen behavior had to go!

What was his calling? Wasn't it to insure the survival of the children of Israel and the rest of the world during the upcoming famine? He was called to serve mankind and was placed in a position of authority to do so. His gifts operated as needed to guide him through the maze of trying and testing to prepare him to properly fulfill the calling on his life. The dream itself was not the calling but the catalyst to put him on the path to fulfillment.

Paul understood his calling and its ramifications since he had been the chief enemy of Jesus' disciples and had been given a corrective interview with Jesus. Before his encounter with Jesus, Paul understood the Mosaic Law but after his encounter he understood the motivation behind the Law- Love. Rather than killing his enemy, Jesus converted his enemy by Love. Paul had a covenant with The Father but until that encounter, he did not understand his calling. For his calling to be fulfilled, it was necessary for Jesus to appear to him. That is not always the case even though we all would enjoy a similar encounter. Paul's calling included writing two thirds of the New Testament under the inspiration of the Holy Spirit. Paul understood that each of us has a purpose and a covenant as he wrote the following:

Rom 12:1-5:

1 I beseech you therefore, brethren, by the mercies of God, that ye present your bodies a living sacrifice, holy, acceptable unto God, [which is] your reasonable service.

2 And be not conformed to this world: but be ye transformed by the renewing of your mind, that ye may prove what [is] that good, and acceptable, and perfect, will of God.

3 For I say, through the grace given unto me, to every man that is among you, not to think [of himself] more highly than he ought to think; but to think soberly, according as God hath dealt to every man the measure of faith.

4 For as we have many members in one body, and all members have not the same office:

5 So we, [being] many, are one body in Christ, and every one members one of another. (KJV)

• As we ponder these words with respect to our covenant, we are given instructions for developing our covenant:

• Present your body as a living, acceptable sacrifice

• Be not conformed to the ways of the world

• Be transformed by renewing your mind to the good, acceptable, and perfect will of God

• Do not think of yourself more highly than you ought to think

• Think soberly, be moderate and in self-control

• You have been given special and unique advantages according to your covenant with The Father; pursue your covenant and you will gain greater clarity of these advantages.

Chapter 21

THE MOUNT OF TRANSFIGURATION

*A*ll men want power in some fashion but the problem is that they want control also. In the physical realm power and control seem to go hand in hand. Historically, men who have gained power were not guided by Love. When Love is in command, power is good whereas power in the hands of "control" is bad.

In the ninth chapter of Mark, Jesus pointed to an end result of Love in command. He started out with the following words, "I tell you the truth, there are some standing here who will not experience death before they see the kingdom of God come with power."

What did Jesus just say? He eluded to a truth and mystery that many have missed. "The kingdom of God with POWER" would be what every Christian wanted to see. The earth has yearned for the time when the kingdom of God would prevail over all the worldly sin and perverseness that is ever increasing.

Let's examine Mark 9:2: "Six days later, Jesus took with him Peter, James, and John and led them alone up a high mountain privately. And he was transfigured before them."

"Six days" frequently refers to the six thousand year reign prior to the millennium. A high mountain is symbolic of a kingdom and Jesus wanted to privately show his closest disciples what he was eluding to in verse one. The fullness of the kingdom is tied directly to a power that supersedes the world of structure. Jesus had full and complete command and authority over his physical body prior to the cross and resurrection.

The next verse reveals additional clues to this power: "And his raiment became shining, exceeding white as snow; so as no fuller on earth can white them". Jesus' clothes also took on this transfigured state rather than concealing it. All of the molecules making up his clothes were under his command. This power was transmitted to his clothes just as the widow revealed this phenomenon when she touched the hem of his garment. This demonstration of power was impressive and by itself was sufficient to make the point with the three disciples (or witnesses) without any further display. But there's more.

"And there appeared unto them Elias with Moses: and they were talking with Jesus." Now we have really taken this power to the limit, Elijah and Moses have showed up on the scene in full display of the disciples and they were talking with Jesus as well! This verse has tremendous ramifications yet Christians have missed the implications of this Scripture throughout the age. Could it be that this is the time of revealing? Just as the disciples were shown this revelation after six days are we being shown the fullness of this revelation after six thousand years? The mere fact that our focus is placed on this passage is an indication that The Father may allow us to unlock the mystery given to us to understand.

Why Elijah and Moses? Elijah represented the Spirit of God and Moses represented the Law of God but first on the scene in his transfigured or glorified state was Jesus who represented the Love of God. Both the Spirit and the Law are encompassed by the Love of God. Love summons both the manifestation of the Spirit and the Law. Neither have died but are eternal. The Law was not done away with but fulfilled when Love became flesh as our example, Jesus. The Law could not be fulfilled without Love and the fruit of this fulfillment is grace and mercy.

How did the disciples respond to this supernatural display? Never with a loss for words, Peter provides a second witness to the unlocking of this mystery as well as the timing, "Master, it is good for us to be here: and let us make three tabernacles; one for thee, and one for Moses, and one for Elias." The Feast of Tabernacles completes the three feast cycle: Passover, Pentecost, and Tabernacles. Elijah (or John) provided hope. Moses provided faith (the giving of the Law to be heard), and Jesus provided Love. Faith, hope, and Love all came together in a glorified state and pointed us to that third and final feast- Tabernacles.

There are other truths found in this passage. Elijah and Moses were not dead, they are alive. The disciples were able to recognize them by some form of communication. They could hear Elijah and Moses talking to Jesus. Jesus knew them as well. Could you imagine being there during this supernatural display by the Son of the Most High God?

How could he be transfigured before his crucifixion? What revelation did Jesus have that has defied our understanding? Is this state available to us prior to death?

"And there was a cloud that overshadowed them: and a voice came out of the cloud, saying, This is my beloved Son: hear him. " To top it all off, Our Heavenly Father manifested in a cloud and was heard in an audible form. Notice that HE did not focus on the Law or the Prophets but only on Jesus. Jesus fulfilled the Law and the Prophets by adding the one missing ingredient- Love. As Paul shared in 1 Corinthians: "But when that which is perfect has come, then that which is in part will be done away."

Once the revelation was given, Elijah, Moses, and the manifestation of Our Heavenly Father were gone. Here we have three witnesses required to establish truth. This is a law given to Moses in Deuteronomy 17 and reiterated by Jesus in Matthew 18, "in the mouth of two or three witnesses every word may be established." The three disciples were shown the event but without full understanding. Their job was to faithfully communicate what they saw, but only after the resurrection. They were more focused on the "rising from the dead" than the fact that Jesus had the power to operate in a transfigured state which clearly supersedes all of the natural laws we have assumed to be in control over our physical bodies.

The disciples were instructed to listen to Jesus. The first question Jesus responded to was the Elijah question concerning the restoration of all things. In verse 13 Jesus told them that Elijah had certainly come and was referring to

John the Baptist's ministry. Elijah's ministry had been cut short by three and one half years. He performed eight miracles whereas Elisha performed sixteen miracles. A full rest cycle is seven days, seven years, or seven thousand years. Jesus reveals that John the Baptist was the greatest of the prophets and the culmination of the prophecies by the law and the prophets was at hand:

Matthew 11:12: And from the days of John the Baptist until now the kingdom of heaven suffereth violence, and the violent take it by force. 13 For all the prophets and the law prophesied until John. 14 And if ye will receive [it], this is Elias, which was for to come. 15 He that hath ears to hear, let him hear.

What is required to restore all things? Love.

Chapter 22

THE BIG PICTURE

*T*here have been many facets of understanding about the Key of David.

1Samuel 13:14:

"But now your kingdom shall not continue. The LORD has sought for Himself a man after His own heart, and the LORD has commanded him to be commander over His people, because you have not kept what the LORD commanded you."

Isaiah 22:22:

And the key of the house of David will I lay upon his shoulder; so he shall open, and none shall shut; and he shall shut, and none shall open.

Revelations 3:7-8:

7 And to the angel of the church in Philadelphia write; These things saith he that is holy, he that is true, he that hath the key of David, he that openeth, and no man shutteth; and

shutteth, and no man openeth;8 I know thy works: behold, I have set before thee an open door, and no man can shut it: for thou hast a little strength, and hast kept my word, and hast not denied my name.

I believe the Key of David is a direct reference to unlocking the revelation of Love in our hearts. David was clearly human and dealt with the flesh just as we all do. However, he was known as the man who was after Our Heavenly Father's own heart:

Act 13:21-23:

21 And afterward they desired a king: and God gave unto them Saul the son of Cis, a man of the tribe of Benjamin, by the space of forty years.

22 And when he had removed him, he raised up unto them David to be their king; to whom also he gave testimony, and said, I have found David the [son] of Jesse, a man after mine own heart, which shall fulfil all my will.

23 Of this man's seed hath God according to [his] promise raised unto Israel a Saviour, Jesus: (KJV)

The only quality mentioned of David centered around Love, not his qualities as a king, warrior, husband, or father. The qualification of Love is mentioned in the same sentence with the fulfillment of Our Heavenly Father's will. This attribute was to be passed down (in his seed) to bring forth the promised savior: Jesus. I believe that as we corporately grasp this revelation that has been hidden in plain sight, we will enter into the millennium of rest spoken of in Scripture. A new level of creativity will emerge and solutions to global problems will surface and be implemented. Simplicity will replace complexity. Resources will no longer be controlled by a select few but all of mankind will reap the rewards of the Love of Our Heavenly Father being manifested on earth as it is in Heaven. This Love will permeate every aspect of life and man's motivation will be one of service for his brother and Our Lord's Prayer will be fully realized.

Now that you have begun to focus on a life of Love, reread the revelation of Love that Our Heavenly Father has placed before us:

1 Corinthians 13:

THOUGH I speak with the tongues of men and of angels, but have not love, I have become sounding brass or a clanging cymbal.

And though I have the gift of prophecy, and understand all mysteries and all knowledge, and though I have all faith, so that I could remove mountains, but have not love, I am nothing.

And though I bestow all my goods to feed the poor, and though I give my body to be burned, but have not love, it profits me nothing.

Love suffers long and is kind; love does not envy; love does not parade itself, is not puffed up; does not behave rudely, does not seek its own, is not provoked, thinks no evil; does not rejoice in iniquity, but rejoices in the truth; bears all things, believes all things, hopes all things, endures all things.

Love never fails. But whether there are prophecies, they will fail; whether there are tongues, they will cease; whether there is knowledge, it will vanish away.

For we know in part and we prophesy in part.

But when that which is perfect has come, then that which is in part will be done away.

When I was a child, I spoke as a child, I understood as a child, I thought as a child; but when I became a man, I put away childish things.

For now we see in a mirror, dimly, but then face to face. Now I know in part, but then I shall know just as I also am known.

And now abide faith, hope, love, these three; but the greatest of these is love. (NKJV)

I end with this question: Are you to going to be known as a person after Our Heavenly Father's own heart?